REVISED EDITION

Dining In–Kansas City

COOKBOOK

D1027064

REVISED EDITION

Dining In–Kansas City

COOKBOOK

A Collection of Gourmet Recipes for Complete Meals
from Kansas City's Finest Restaurants

BOOTS MATHEWS
and
JAMES RIEGER

Foreword by
HENRY BLOCH

Peanut Butter Publishing
Mercer Island, Washington

TITLES IN SERIES

Cover photograph by Bob Barrett Photography, Kansas City,
    Missouri. (Food courtesy of Harry Starker's Restaurant)
Edited by Charles Malody
Production and Illustration by Carol Naumann
Typesetting by Mac White-Spunner & April Ryan

Copyright © 1983 by Peanut Butter Publishing,
2445 76th Avenue S.E., Mercer Island, WA 98040
All rights reserved. Printed in the United States of America.
ISBN 0-89716-127-0

DEDICATION

This book is dedicated to the 50th Anniversary of the Nelson-Atkins Museum of Art.

CONTENTS

INTRODUCTION

Everyone knows that cooking is an art. But not everyone realizes that eating, too, is an art. The art of eating, of course, requires discrimination and a keen sense for nuances. Moreover, the true eater is curious and adventuresome. He shuns narrowness in the quest of delight and inform his palate. Fried chicken and salmon mousse are equal and without prejudice in the mind of the true eater.

There is a maxim in the art world that says one can gauge a connoisseur's understanding and love of art by the way he eats. There is more than a little truth in that saying. The true connoisseur, whether collector or curator, is relentless in the pursuit of what is really good and in rejecting the shoddy. Demanding—yes. Pretentious and prejudiced—never.

Since this book is dedicated to the 50th Anniversary of the Nelson-Atkins Museum of Art in 1983, it seems appropriate to recall the philosophy that has made the Nelson-Atkins one of the nation's major art museums in a short fifty years.

Our business first and foremost is about art. Great works of art embody an important portion of mankind's genius and reveal ways in which we have viewed ourselves and the world about us. They put us in touch with other people from other places and other times, thus expanding our horizons and enriching our experience. The great work of art stimulates and brings enjoyment.

Our finest educational triumph is to establish an informed encounter between a work of art and the visitor. The way we present works of art bears on that encounter, either hindering it or helping it. Ultimately all our educational programs, whether for the young or old, experienced or inexperienced, aim at making sure that the dialogue between the work of art and the individual is an informed one. And it should be an enjoyable one, too. We are about enjoyment—the delight to be found in art.

It follows, then, that our prime act of public service is to bring works of art of supreme quality to Kansas City. Works of art are permanent resources that will be here for generation after generation to learn from and to enjoy.

William Rockhill Nelson said it well when he specified that his funds be used to acquire works of art "which will contribute to the delectation and enjoyment of the public generally."

Over the brief fifty-year history of the Museum, we have been served by devoted trustees, staff, and supporters who have understood the fundamental values that make an art museum great and of real service to its community. They have had the wisdom and courage to stick to those values, even when passing tides of fashion made it difficult to do so. The philosophy has served us well. It has been the key to a phenomenally successful past. And it will be the key to a brilliant future.

Marc F. Wilson
Director, Nelson-Atkins
Museum of Art

FOREWORD

Dining can be much more than a routine provision of nutrition we must have; dining can be an art form, a celebration of the sensory appeal of the color, shape, taste, and texture of food. As we dine, we can enjoy varied serving rituals, beautiful surroundings, and perhaps the stimulating conversation of friends and business associates, all while savoring the varied simple-to-elaborate foods which are part of the dining experience.

As a founder and President of H&R Block, I have traveled extensively from Kansas City to many other parts of our country and the world. Some of my strongest and most pleasant memories are associated with new foods and dining experiences while traveling. Yet, when I return to Kansas City, I rediscover the joy and the imcomparable pleasure of dining here. Perhaps one must travel to other places to fully appreciate the quality and diversity of the Kansas City restaurants.

Kansas City is world famous for its steaks, barbecue, and fried chicken. But, restaurants featuring ethnic specialties, haute cuisine, and assorted other fine foods, served in beautiful picturesque surroundings continue to prosper and abound in our city.

Dining In–Kansas City identifies some of the outstanding restaurants—ones which you should visit with friends or out-of-town visitors. You can always count on an enjoyable and memorable occasion. In addition, this book enables each of us to appreciate the care and skill involved in the preparation of the delicious foods we choose when dining out. The generosity of gifted chefs and restaurant staffs provide these treasured recipes that will give you the opportunity to prepare and serve a chef's favorite dish when you dine at home.

As you set forth on the fabulous adventure of dining out or in, remember that great food and its serving is in part an art form. It is thus most appropriate that this new edition of *Dining In–Kansas City* be dedicated to the 50th birthday of the Nelson-Atkins Museum of Art, which will benefit from the sale of this book.

Henry W. Bloch

alameda plaza

Dinner for Four

Escargots à la Maison

Limaise Salad with Honey Lime Dressing

Watercress Finger Sandwiches

Watermelon Sorbet

Veal Oscar

Tomato Crustade

Flan with Sauce Melba

Wines:

With Escargots—Michelle Redde Pouilly Fumé

With Limaise Salad—Bernkastle Riesling

Troken Sekt, Dr. Thanisch

With Veal Chop—Rutherford Hill Merlot

With Flan—Chateau Larressingle Armagnac

John Lombardo, Manager/Food and Beverage Director

Tariq Khan, Food and Beverage Manager

Jess Barbosa, Executive Chef

ALAMEDA PLAZA ROOF RESTAURANT

The Alameda Plaza Roof Restaurant is atop the Alameda Plaza Hotel. The hotel, which opened in 1972, has in a few short years acquired an international reputation as one of America's outstanding luxury hotels. One gets a spectacular view of Kansas City's Country Club Plaza on the way up to the restaurant via the hotel's all-glass exterior elevator.

The Spanish/Moorish architecture and decor of the Country Club Plaza pervades the mood of the Alameda Plaza Roof Restaurant. Dark, heavy beams, high ceilings and wrought-iron decorative accessories complement the architecture. The predominant colors are warm oranges and reds with burnt-orange tablecloths. There is a formal air to the dining room, but it is not stiff. Windows along the north and south sides of the dining room give a beautiful view of the Country Club Plaza night or day. The seating ranges from comfortable, intimate booths, to small tables for two or more, on up to large round tables for parties of ten.

The food is the result of a congenial team of two: John Lombardo, Manager and Food & Beverage Director, and Jess Barbosa, Executive Chef. John Lombardo started as a dishwasher and busboy at the age of fourteen. Since that early beginning, he has trained in every area from baking to tableside cooking. Chef Barbosa got his culinary start courtesy of the United States Navy. He has come a long way since those days. At the Alameda he is running a large commercial kitchen but with the personal attention and pride of the master chef. Not a detail escapes his eye. Jess and John both emphasize the importance of top-quality ingredients to get good results.

The Alameda Plaza Roof Restaurant has been awarded the Ivy Award by *Institutions*, the Silver Spoon Award by *Outlook*, and honored for having one of the Top 100 Wine Lists by *Wine Spectator*. The restaurant offers a table d'hôte menu each night in addition to a wide range of menu items at lunch and dinner.

Wornall Road at Ward Parkway   756-1500

WATERCRESS FINGER SANDWICHES

4 *slices white bread*
1 *bunch watercress*

2 *tablespoons mayonnaise*
Salt and pepper

1. Trim crust off bread, then butter each slice.
2. Wash watercress, then chop very fine.
3. Add mayonnaise and seasoning to watercress; mix thoroughly.
4. Spread watercress mixture on two slices of the bread, and top with remaining slices.
5. Cut sandwiches in half, serve garnished with watercress.

WATERMELON SORBET

1 *quart watermelon pulp*   2 *tablespoons lime juice*
⅓ *cup sugar*

1. Put watermelon pulp in food processor or blender, and puree.
2. Dissolve sugar in lime juice.
3. Combine watermelon and sugar-lime mixture, place in ice-cream freezer and follow operating instructions. Yield: 1 quart.

   Optional: You may add two beaten egg whites to mixture in ice-cream freezer, after it starts to freeze. This will give you a consistency similar to a sherbet.

VEAL OSCAR

4 (6–7 ounce) veal chops	12–16 asparagus spears
Flour	4 ounces crabmeat, leg
Salt and pepper	chunks
2 tablespoons butter	FOYOT SAUCE

1. Preheat oven to 325°.
2. Flour chops and sprinkle with salt and pepper.
3. Lightly sauté chops brown on each side in butter.
4. Place chops in a greased baking dish, and place uncovered in oven for 15–20 minutes.
5. Apply finger pressure to center of chop; when firm remove from oven.
6. Steam asparagus while veal is cooking.
7. On individual plates, place one veal chop, Tomato Crustade, and 3–4 asparagus spears.
8. Place 1 ounce of crabmeat on top of each veal chop.
9. Mask chop with Foyot Sauce and serve.

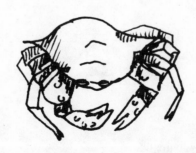

FOYOT SAUCE

2 tablespoons chopped shallots
2 tablespoons tarragon vinegar
5–7 peppercorns, crushed
2 tablespoons white wine
3 egg yolks

¾ pound clarified butter
½ lemon (juice only)
2 tablespoons strong beef consommé
Salt to taste
Few grains of cayenne
½ tarragon leaf, chopped

1. Reduce the chopped shallots, tarragon vinegar and crushed peppercorns until almost dry.
2. Add wine and egg yolks. Beat the mixture to thick, creamy consistency using either low heat or water bath.
3. Maintaining very low heat, mix in melted butter very slowly, beating constantly.
4. Add lemon juice, consommé, salt and pepper.
5. Strain through cheese cloth.
6. Garnish with chopped tarragon leaves.

To clarify butter:
Cut the butter into pieces and place in a saucepan over moderate heat. When the butter has melted, skim off the foam, and strain the clear yellow liquid into a bowl, leaving the milky residue in the bottom of the pan. The clear yellow liquid is the clarified butter.

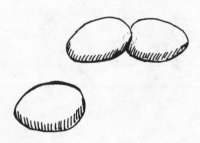

TOMATO CRUSTADE

2 medium-size tomatoes
3 ounces cream cheese (at room temperature)
1 tablespoon fresh chives
⅛ teaspoon white pepper
⅛ teaspoon salt
2 tablespoons Parmesan cheese

2 tablespoons bread crumbs
2 tablespoons flour
1 cup egg wash (2 eggs to a ½ cup milk—season with salt and white pepper)
¼ pound butter
Paprika

1. Slice the tomatoes, making sure you have four even slices out of each tomato.
2. Mix cream cheese, chives, salt and white pepper thoroughly until smooth.
3. Lay tomato slices on flat surface, spreading cream cheese on four of the slices. Place a plain tomato slice on top of each covered slice, so that the cream cheese is in the middle.
4. Mix Parmesan cheese and bread crumbs together. Coat tomatoes with flour, dip in egg wash, then in bread crumb mixture.
5. Sauté on medium heat in butter until golden brown.
6. Garnish with paprika.

FLAN MELBA

1 pint half & half	1 teaspoon vanilla extract
4 eggs (extra large)	2 tablespoons water
⅛ teaspoon salt	SAUCE MELBA
1 cup sugar	

1. Preheat oven to 325°.
2. Heat half & half to boiling point.
3. Beat the eggs. Add ½ cup sugar and salt and mix thoroughly. Do not aerate! Add the hot half & half. Stir in vanilla. Strain.
4. Heat ½ cup sugar in a heavy pan over low heat. Stir constantly with a wooden spoon until sugar is melted. Remove pan from heat and add water *very slowly* and *carefully* (adding water quickly can be very dangerous and may cause an explosive reaction). Return the pan to low heat and cook until mixture is golden brown. (If using a candy thermometer 122°R or 306.5°F)
5. Coat the sides of four custard cups with butter, then pour ¼ of caramelized sugar into bottom of cup.
6. Pour custard mixture into custard cups. Place the cups in a pan of hot, but not boiling, water. Poach in oven for approximately 30–35 minutes.
7. To test for doneness, insert the tip of a knife into custard near the edge of the cup. If the blade comes out clean, the custard should be removed from the oven and water bath. There is sufficient heat stored in the custard and the cup to complete the cooking process after removal from the oven. The custard will be firm in the center by the time it has cooled.
8. Invert the custard cup onto a platter or individual dessert dishes. The liquid caramel will flow down sides of the custard. If custard is thoroughly chilled, it may be necessary to dip cups approximately ½ inch into hot water (dip very quickly) so that syrup will be released.
9. Decorate as desired, served with Sauce Melba.

ALAMEDA PLAZA ROOF RESTAURANT

SAUCE MELBA

14 ounces raspberries, fresh
   or frozen

½ cup confectioner's sugar
1 tablespoon lemon juice

1. Puree raspberries. Transfer to saucepan and add sugar. Bring quickly to a boil.
2. Cool and add the lemon juice. Yield: 1 pint.

NOTE: For a winter version of Sauce Melba, combine in a saucepan:
   ¼ cup raspberry jam
   2 tablespoons sugar
   ½ cup water
Stir and boil for 2 minutes. Cool and add 1 tablespoon lemon juice.

AMERICAN RESTAURANT

Dinner for Six

Sirloin Steak, Thin and Raw, with Mustard-Parmesan Dressing

Sautéed Shrimp in Fennel Butter, with Shrimp Fritters

Great Grandmother's Wild Greens

Sugarbrush Mountain Maple Mousse

Wines:

With appetizer–Cabernet Sauvignon, Joseph Heitz Cellars, 1979

With main course–Fumé Blanc, Robert Mondavi, 1981

Ken Dunn, Chef

Rolf Wetzel, Director

Richard King, President

Most people, if they heard that a restaurant was serving American food, would, without hesitation, imagine the menu to consist of fried chicken, cheeseburgers, barbecued ribs, onion rings and apple pie. They would certainly be mistaken in the case of the American Restaurant.

The American Restaurant, perched on top of Hall's at Crown Center has a better idea. It serves American regional cuisine with offerings such as: Poached Spiny Lobster in White Wine with Blue Corn Tortillas, Mignons of Beef Flared in Bourbon, Great Grandmother's Wild Greens and Sea Scallops Simmered in Mustard Cream with Orange and Lime Zest. "American cookery, the way we do it, is as fine a cuisine as one can find," asserts Richard King, president of American Foodservice Enterprises, which operates the American. "We purchase only the freshest of the fresh at the time it comes into season and especially use light sauces and fresh herbs in preparing both the creative and the authentic."

Moreover, most people, if they heard that an architect had designed an American restaurant, would simply imagine the interior to resemble a colonial dining room or a frontiersman's rugged cabin. In surprise, they would marvel at what New Haven architect Warren Platner has done for the American Restaurant. The American is spectacular. The ceiling in the main dining room, which is over three stories high, is covered with a fan-shaped network of wood and clear lights. The carpeting, the shutters on the ceiling-high windows, and the napery are shades of beige, all highlighted by scarlet banquettes.

"Yet, as beautiful as the restaurant is, the emphasis falls on food," says Ken Dunn, executive chef of the American Restaurant. "Above all, people dine out for the food first and then the service and atmosphere. If the food meets their expectations, they will return."

200 East 25th Street   471-8050

SIRLOIN STEAK, THIN AND RAW, WITH MUSTARD-PARMESAN DRESSING

2 egg yolks
1 tablespoon chopped garlic
 Freshly ground black
  pepper
¾ tablespoon Maille
  mustard
1 teaspoon salt
1 teaspoon Worchestershire
  sauce

¼ cup tarragon vinegar
1 cup olive oil
1 cup grated Parmesan
  cheese
1 pound strip sirloin,
  trimmed of all fat, sliced
  very thin

1. Combine egg yolks, garlic, black pepper, Maille mustard, and salt in a blender. Blend well.
2. In a small bowl, combine Worchestershire sauce, vinegar, and olive oil. Slowly blend with egg yolk mixture to create a mayonnaise.
3. When mayonnaise is completed, fold in ½ cup grated Parmesan cheese.
4. Place sirloin slices in a fan arrangement on six 10-inch dinner plates, with slices barely overlapping.
5. Spoon mustard-Parmesan dressing over the bottom center of the fanned sirloin slices.
6. Combine remaining Parmesan cheese and parsley. Sprinkle mixture in a horizontal arc over the center of each plate of fanned raw sirloin. Serve immediately.

NOTE: This can be used as an hors d'oeuvre by rolling meat individually and skewering and then dipping into mustard-Parmesan dressing.

Ask your butcher for a tender, well-aged pound of strip sirloin. Ask him to remove all fat and to slice it very thin. (He may want to freeze it first for slicing ease.) Refrigerate the steak.

SAUTÉED SHRIMP IN FENNEL BUTTER

2 cups white wine
3 shallots, minced
4 garlic cloves, minced
2 teaspoons whole
   peppercorns
¾ pound unsalted butter,
   room temperature
2 teaspoons ground fennel
   seed

¼ teaspoon Worcestershire
   sauce
1 teaspoon garlic powder
1 teaspoon Kosher salt
¾ cup Pernod liqueur
30 large shrimp, peeled,
   deveined and butterflied
Juice of 3 lemons
Salt and pepper
SHRIMP FRITTERS

1. Combine wine, shallots, garlic, and peppercorns in saucepan and bring to a boil. Reduce heat and simmer for 20–25 minutes, reducing liquid to one-third. Cool to room temperature, strain and cream into one-half pound of butter.
2. Combine fennel, Worcestershire, garlic powder, salt, and 2 tablespoons Pernod and mix well into butter mixture.
3. Melt remaining butter in a large saucepan. Add shrimp and sauté for 4 minutes or until shrimp turns pink.
4. Add remaining Pernod to shrimp and cook on medium heat for 3 minutes. Add 1 cup of Fennel Butter into shrimp mixture, melt and combine well.
5. Add lemon juice and combine with shrimp mixture. Season with salt and pepper to taste.
6. Remove shrimp, place on plates or serving platter. Pour Fennel Butter over shrimp and serve with Fritters.

AMERICAN RESTAURANT

SHRIMP FRITTERS

¼ cup carrots, grated
1 teaspoon ground pepper
1½ cups flour
1 teaspoon sugar
2 teaspoons paprika

2 teaspoons Kosher salt
1 bottle beer
Juice of one lemon
16 shrimp, peeled, deveined, diced into ½" pieces

1. Combine all ingredients but shrimp into a batter.
2. Fold shrimp lightly into batter. Fry in deep fat for approximately 5 minutes, or until golden brown.

NOTE: If you desire to flame the shrimp, as we do over a gas flame, add the Pernod, heat for 20 or so seconds and tilt pan into flame, igniting mixture.

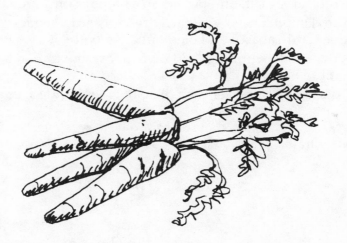

GREAT GRANDMOTHER'S WILD GREENS

1 bunch each: turnip, mustard, and collard greens
2 medium-size onions, finely chopped
2 medium-size tomatoes, peeled, seeded and finely chopped
3 cloves garlic, minced
2 teaspoons Kosher salt

1 teaspoon freshly ground black pepper
1 teaspoon fresh lemon juice
¾ cup white wine vinegar
1 tablespoon dry mustard
¼ cup sugar
½ tablespoon Worcestershire sauce
½ tablespoon Tabasco sauce
1½ cups salad oil

1. Stem and wash all greens, and dry them with a tea towel. Tear or cut them into bite-sized pieces. Divide into six equal portions and place on chilled salad plates.
2. Combine onions and tomatoes. Mix well. Divide into six equal portions and place atop center of each plate of greens.
3. Whip garlic, salt, and pepper in a blender until smooth.
4. Add lemon juice, vinegar, dry mustard, sugar, Worcestershire sauce and Tabasco and blend until smooth.
5. With blender running, add oil to above mixture in a steady stream until all is combined.
6. Drizzle dressing over each plate of greens and serve at once.

NOTE: Try adding chopped hard-cooked eggs and bacon for additional flavoring and presentation.

SUGARBRUSH MOUNTAIN MAPLE MOUSSE

2 eggs, separated
½ cup pure maple syrup
1 teaspoon maple extract
¼ cup dark brown sugar
¾ tablespoons Knox gelatin

¼ cup cold water
1 cup heavy cream, chilled
¾ teaspoon vanilla extract
VANILLA CREAM
RUM SAUCE

1. Place egg whites into stainless steel bowl and put in a warm part of the kitchen.
2. Combine and mix egg yolks, maple syrup, maple extract, and brown sugar in a stainless steel bowl and either place over a pot of boiling water or in a double boiler. Cook until mixture thickens and slightly coats the back of a spoon (approximately 10 minutes). Remove from the heat and cool.
3. Stir gelatin in cold water and cook over moderate heat to dissolve the gelatin thoroughly. Remove from the heat and add slowly to the maple mixture, stirring constantly to incorporate the gelatin. Let cool.
4. With a wire whisk, rotary or electric beater, whip the chilled cream in a large chilled stainless steel bowl until it is firm enough to hold its shape, then add vanilla extract. Set whipped cream aside.

5. Beat the egg whites into fluffy, soft peaks. Fold into the maple mixture, then fold in whipped cream.

6. Place into molds, about the size of a coffee cup, and refrigerate for 2 to 4 hours or until set.

7. When ready to serve, unmold by dipping into hot water for a few seconds. Turn upside down on a serving plate. Spoon Vanilla Rum Sauce over mousse.

AMERICAN RESTAURANT

VANILLA CREAM RUM SAUCE

1 cup heavy cream
1 cup milk
2 tablespoons dark rum
¼ cup plus 2 tablespoons
    sugar

2 egg yolks
1 teaspoon vanilla
2 teaspoons cornstarch
½ teaspoon salt

1. Heat cream, milk, and rum in a double boiler until steaming.
2. Combine remaining ingredients and slowly add to the hot cream mixture. Let cook for 5 minutes or until thickened. Cool and serve with mousse.

NOTE: *When you add the egg mixture to the cream, it is important to temper it first. To temper the eggs, heat them somewhat by spooning some of the cream mixture into them. This reduces the chances of scrambling the eggs when adding them to the hot cream mixture.*

LA BONNE AUBERGE

Dinner for Six

Mousse de Saumon aux Ecrevisses

Sorbet au Champagne

Côtes de Veau aux Morilles

Tomate aux Concombres à la Crème

Timbale Elysée

Wines:

With Mousse—a Chablis

With Veal—a Médoc

Gus Riedi, Owner and Chef

"It has been a struggle," recounts an amused Gus Riedi, speaking of his fervent effort to operate an outstanding French restaurant in Kansas City. The chef-owner of La Bonne Auberge, Gus, like a Swiss Horatio Alger, started at the bottom. When he arrived in Kansas City, a penniless foreigner, he spoke fluent French and German, but no English; and although he had apprenticed as a chef in Switzerland at sixteen, his first job in town at the Muehlbach Hotel required that he merely peel Dover Sole and cut onions throughout the day.

After the Muehlbach he worked in a number of restaurants, among them the Kansas City Club and Le Châteaubriand, before opening a coffee shop in North Kansas City. "That was all I could afford back then," remembers Gus, a highly skilled chef who can make pâte en croute in his sleep. "We had a steam table and made sandwiches. It was really something." In time he converted the coffee shop to a French restaurant. Since then he has been steadily improving the quality of his restaurant, and he now feels he will overcome his history of bad locations in his new 51st and Main quarters.

The new La Bonne Auberge serves many nouvelle cuisine dishes, which Gus characterizes as lighter, simpler fare than traditional French food. "Nouvelle cuisine has thinner sauces with little or no starch, unusual combinations of food, slightly underdone vegetables and carefully arranged oversize plates."

Yet, while his cooking may change, Gus has not. "I still want to have an excellent French restaurant, as good as any in Chicago or New York. We're about there."

51st and Main

MOUSSE DE SAUMON AUX ECREVISSES

6 large shrimp, shelled and
   cleaned (reserve shells)
¾ pound salmon
   Salt and white pepper

2 egg whites
1½ cups cream
   SHRIMP SAUCE

1. Preheat oven to 350°. Butter six individual soufflé ramekins. Cube the raw shrimp and salmon. Season both with salt and pepper.
2. Put the salmon in a food processor. As you process it, add the egg whites, then slowly add the cream. If necesary, add more seasoning to taste.
3. Fold the cubed shrimp into the salmon mixture. Spoon the mousse into the ramekins.
4. Place the ramekins in a pan of almost-boiling water. (The water should come halfway up the sides of the ramekins.) Cover loosely with foil and bake 12 to 15 minutes. Test for doneness by inserting a toothpick into the mousse. If it comes out clean, the mousse has cooked enough.
5. Unmold the mousse and serve with Shrimp Sauce.

The fresher the salmon, the greater its binding power and the more cream it will hold. The more cream it holds, the smoother the mousse. The cream should be very cold for this recipe so that the salmon can hold it more easily.

SHRIMP SAUCE

6 shrimp shells (from salmon mousse), or more if available
1½ tablespoons butter
1 teaspoon tomato paste

1 shallot, minced
¼ cup white wine
½ cup clam juice
1 cup cream
1 teaspoon lemon juice

1. Sauté the shells in butter until they are rose-colored. Add the tomato paste and shallot.
2. Add the wine and clam juice. Reduce by half. Strain the liquid into another saucepan.
3. Add cream to shrimp liquid and reduce the sauce to a syrup consistency.
4. Taste for seasoning. Add salt if necessary, but be careful with it because the clam juice is salty. Stir in the lemon juice.

SORBET AU CHAMPAGNE

2 cups water	2 tablespoons lemon juice
1 cup sugar	1 bottle of champagne
Peel of ½ lemon	

1. Combine water, sugar, lemon peel, and juice. Stir over low heat until sugar is dissolved. Bring to a boil and boil for 5 minutes. Cool for 2 hours. Strain out the peel.
2. Add half the champagne (keeping the other half well-corked in the ice box or on ice) and freeze the mixture in an ice-cream freezer according to the manufacturer's instructions.
3. Place in a closed container and set in the freezer for about 2 hours.
4. Serve in cooled wine glasses. Pour the rest of the champagne over.

This amount of sorbet is too much for six people but in my opinion it would be very hard to freeze a smaller quantity. Sorbet served in this manner takes the place of what used to be called the "trou du milieu" or a refreshing respite between courses. It played a more important role when dinners consisted of ten to twelve courses.

COTES DE VEAU AUX MORILLES

3 ounces dried morilles
   (mushrooms)

6 veal chops, cut thick—
   at least ½",
   preferably ¾"
   Flour seasoned with salt
   and pepper

4 tablespoons clarified
   butter

1 tablespoon finely minced
   shallots

¼ cup brandy

½ cup white wine

¾ cup cream

1. Soak the mushrooms in several changes of cold water, gently washing them after they have softened. (Grit usually clings to them.) Cut into bite-size pieces.
2. Dredge the veal chops in the flour. Shake off excess. Sauté in the butter about 3 minutes per side, making sure not to burn the butter. Remove the veal and keep warm.
3. Add the shallots to pan. As soon as they cease foaming, add the brandy. Reduce mixture by half.
4. Add the wine and again reduce by half. Strain out the shallots and veal settings. Add cream to the strained mixture. Reduce to a thick syrup. Add the mushrooms and bring to a boil. Taste for seasoning.
5. Return veal to the pan, adding any juices that the chops may have left. As soon as veal is hot, serve.

NOTE: The sauce should be brownish beige in color. The veal settings should provide the color. If they don't, add 1 tablespoon of a dark meat flavoring, like Kitchen Bouquet.

TOMATE aux CONCOMBRES à la CRÉME

3 *large tomatoes, halved, or*
  6 small tomatoes
  Salt and pepper to taste
2 *medium-size cucumbers*
  (burpless, if possible)
1 *teaspoon minced shallots*

¼ *teaspoon minced garlic*
  Butter
½ *cup heavy cream*
  White pepper
  Juice of ½ lemon

1. Preheat oven to 350°.
2. Scoop out the centers of the tomato halves (or small tomatoes). Season shells with salt and pepper and turn upside down to drain.
3. Peel cucumbers, remove seeds, and cut into cubes or shape them like garlic cloves. Blanch in boiling salted water and drain.
4. Sauté the shallots and garlic in butter. Add cucumbers to the skillet, then the cream. Cook until the cream has reduced to a syrupy consistency. Season with salt, white pepper, and a little lemon juice.
5. Heat the tomatoes for 5 minutes in preheated oven, then fill with cucumbers and sauce. Serve hot.

Cucumbers are not usually served hot in this country but they garnish veal and chicken well.

TIMBALE ELYSÉE

¼ cup sugar
2 quarts water
  Juice of 1 lemon
3 fresh peaches, skinned, halves, and pitted
½ cup raspberries
6 tablespoons confectioners' sugar

6 *GÉNOISE CIRCLES*
2 tablespoons kirsch
6 *ALMOND PASTRY CUPS*
1 pint *VANILLA ICE CREAM*
1 cup whipped cream made with 2 tablespoons powdered sugar
6 candied violets

1. Mix sugar, water, and lemon juice and bring to a boil. Poach peach halves over low heat about 5 minutes or until tender.
2. Mash raspberries with confectioners' sugar. Strain.
3. Sprinkle the Genoise Circles with kirsch and place in the bottoms of the Almond Pastry Cups. Cover each with a scoop of Vanilla Ice Cream and a peach half.
4. Spoon 1 tablespoon raspberry sauce over peaches. Top each serving with whipped cream (using a pastry bag with fluted tip) and a candied violet.

GÉNOISE CIRCLES

4 eggs
½ cup sugar
½ teaspoon vanilla

1 cup sifted cake flour
4 tablespoons sweet butter, melted

1. Preheat oven to 325°.
2. Place the eggs, sugar, and vanilla in the top part of a double boiler over hot but not boiling water. Beat with a wire whisk until the mixture is thick and forms a ribbon, 15 to 20 minutes.
3. Remove the egg mixture from heat and whip until cold. Fold in the flour and pour in the melted butter, mixing gently with a spatula.
4. Pour the mixture into a buttered and floured pan, about 10″ square, and bake for 25 minutes in preheated oven. Turn out onto a wire rack and cool.
5. When cool, cut into ½″-thick circles to fit bottoms of pastry cup.

ALMOND PASTRY CUPS

6 ounces almond paste
½ cup sugar
½ cup all-purpose flour

¼ cup milk
2 egg whites, lightly
  whipped

1. Preheat oven to 350°.
2. Mix almond paste, sugar, flour, and milk. Fold in egg whites.
3. With the back of a spoon, spread six rounds of dough as thin as possible, 5-6 inches in diameter, on a buttered and floured baking sheet. Bake 7 to 10 minutes, or until golden brown, in preheated oven.
4. Immediately remove circles one at a time with a spatula, pressing each gently into the bottom of a dessert cup or compote glass. Work as quickly as possible because the pastry loses its flexibility in minutes. When cool, remove from glasses.

LA BONNE AUBERGE

VANILLA ICE CREAM

½ cup milk   5 egg yolks
1 cup heavy cream   ¼ cup sugar
1 vanilla bean   Pinch of salt

1. Bring milk and cream to a boil. Cover and remove from heat.
2. Cut vanilla bean in half and scrape the insides well with a knife. Place scrapings and husks in boiled milk and cream. Let stand covered about 10 minutes.
3. Combine egg yolks, sugar, and salt; whip until foamy. Bring cream mixture back to boil and strain into egg yolk mixture. Return to saucepan and heat slowly, stirring constantly. When mixture thickly coats a wooden spoon (180°), remove from heat.
5. Freeze in ice cream freezer according to manufacturer's instructions.

Dinner for Four

Oysters Thermidor

Vine-ripened Tomato Slices Vinaigrette

Broiled Salmon Steaks with Green Peppercorn Herb Butter

Chocolate Fudge Nut Pie

Wine:

Pouilly Fumé, Le Fort

or

Robert Mondavi Chardonnay

Gilbert/Robinson, Inc., Owners

Tom Hart, Manager

Michael Winkler, Chef

BRISTOL BAR & GRILL

Entering the Bristol Bar & Grill is like stepping into old-world elegance. Heavily leaded glass in the doors at the entrance, a green and white tiled floor in the foyer, dark mahogany paneling, lush palms, and intricate tin ceilings conjure up images of gentlemen of yore meeting for conversation, oysters, port, and a good cigar. Rich green tones prevail throughout. The waiters, busboys, and managers wear dark green aprons or smocks to complete this old-world atmosphere. Interesting paintings softly lighted, art objects, silver, and antique-styled furniture add to the Edwardian air. The magnificent stained-glass skylight in the rear dining room once graced an old English office building.

Bristol Bar & Grill specializes in fresh seafood, flown in daily from the Atlantic, Pacific, and Gulf coasts. Seafood kabobs and fish fillets are broiled over an open mesquite fire, in full view of dining guests, to add a subtle taste without masking the delicate seafood flavor. Kansas City steaks are prepared in the same manner. Fresh lobster, crab, shrimp, and mussels are also featured items. A big attraction in the lounge is the seafood appetizer bar where customers stand while enjoying the food and live entertainment.

A 1982 Silver Spoon Award was presented to Bristol by *Corporate Report* magazine for being one of the Top 10 restaurants in Kansas City . . . an honor which the restaurant has received every year since it opened in 1980.

4740 Jefferson   756-0606

OYSTERS THERMIDOR

16 oysters, shucked, on the
half shell

1 pint THERMIDOR SAUCE
1 tablespoon Parmesan
cheese, grated

1. Arrange the shucked oysters on a medium-size platter and place under the broiler.
2. After oysters begin to curl, top each with 1 ounce of Thermidor Sauce, then top with ¼ teaspoon Parmesan cheese. Return to broiler and broil until filling is hot and Parmesan has browned.
3. Arrange on a large platter and garnish with fresh parsley and lemons.

THERMIDOR SAUCE

5 tablespoons unsalted
butter, softened
⅓ pound onions, minced
6 tablespoons flour
2 cups milk
¼ pound Swiss cheese,
grated
⅛ pound Parmesan cheese,
grated

¼ pound crabmeat, cut in
large dice
2 scallions, thinly sliced
⅓ cup dry white wine
½ teaspoon salt
½ teaspoon white pepper
½ teaspoon dry mustard
Pinch cayenne pepper

1. Place the butter in a saucepan and melt, but DO NOT BROWN.
2. Add the onion to melted butter and sauté until transparent.
3. Add the flour to the onion-butter mix and stir to mix. Cook the roux for 3 minutes, without browning.
4. Add the milk slowly in four additions, stirring well after each addition, to create a smooth sauce. Allow the sauce to come to a full boil, stirring often.
5. After the sauce has boiled, add the cheeses, seafood, scallions, and wine. Bring back to a boil, and whip to incorporate all.
6. After the seafood mixture has come back to a boil, add seasonings and simmer all together for 5 minutes.

VINE-RIPENED TOMATO SLICES VINAIGRETTE

4 fresh leaf lettuce leaves,
  washed

3 large, vine-ripened
  beefsteak tomatoes

1 red onion, sliced into thin
  rings

1 cup VINAIGRETTE
  DRESSING

1. Line each salad plate with a lettuce leaf.
2. Core tomatoes and slice each into four thick slices. Place three slices on each lettuce leaf in a shingled manner.
3. Place several onion rings over the tomato slices and spoon the Vinaigrette over the salads.

NOTE: It is important to use vine-ripened tomatoes for this salad.

This is a simple salad, but it is delicious and at its best if you do use beefsteak tomatoes at room temperature.

BRISTOL BAR & GRILL

VINAIGRETTE DRESSING

2 teaspoons salt
1 teaspoon crushed black
   pepper
1 tablespoon sugar

¼ cup red wine vinegar
1 clove garlic, minced
   very fine
¾ cup salad oil or olive oil

In a small bowl, dissolve the seasonings in the vinegar and add the minced garlic. Whisk in the oil slowly and incorporate completely. Mix well before serving.

If you choose to use olive oil, be sure it is of top quality. For best results, the olive oil and tomato flavors should not conflict.

BROILED SALMON STEAKS
WITH GREEN PEPPERCORN HERB BUTTER

6 (8–10 ounce) salmon
   steaks
¼ cup butter, melted

McCormicks Lemon
  Pepper Seasoning, to
  taste
Knorr-Swiss Aromat
  (yellow-label) to taste

1. Have coals prepared and hot.
2. Season fish by dipping both sides in melted butter and sprinkling with Lemon Pepper and Aromat.
3. Place fish on hot grill, approximately 6–8 inches from coals. Broil for 5–6 minutes on each side or until center bone of salmon steak may be removed easily.
4. Remove from grill and remove center bone and outside skin. Top with Green Peppercorn Herb Butter and serve accompanied by fresh vegetable and steamed new potatoes.

GREEN PEPPERCORN HERB BUTTER

¼ pound unsalted butter,
   room temperature
1 tablespoon fresh parsley,
   chopped
1 tablespoon fresh dill,
   chopped

1 tablespoon fresh lemon
   juice, strained
2 teaspoons green
   peppercorns, mashed
1 tablespoon cognac

1. Allow butter to soften and whip until light.
2. Add remainder of ingredients and blend well.
3. Use butter to top broiled fish and meats.

CHOCOLATE FUDGE NUT PIE

5 tablespoons Hershey's Cocoa	¼ cup plus 1 tablespoon butter, melted
10 tablespoons sugar, granulated	1 teaspoon vanilla extract Dash salt
3 whole eggs	1¼ cups pecans, chopped
⅔ cup light Karo Syrup	1 (10-inch) prepared pie shell, unbaked

1. Preheat oven to 350°.
2. In a mixing bowl measure cocoa, add the sugar and combine well.
3. Add eggs into sugar/cocoa mixture and beat well.
4. Add Karo Syrup and blend well.
5. Add melted butter, vanilla, and salt to cocoa mixture. Blend extremely well until butter is totally absorbed.
6. Stir in the pecans, blending well.
7. Pour into the unbaked pie shell and bake in oven for 25 minutes. Lower oven to 325° and bake 25 minutes more, or until done.
8. Serve with a large dollop of unsweetened whipped cream and grated semi-sweet chocolate.

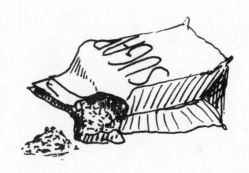

Costello's Greenhouse

Dinner for Four

Crab Rangoon

Caesar Salad

Bouillabaisse

Fruit Fondue

Wine:

Beringer Chenin Blanc

Vince Costello, Owner

COSTELLO'S GREENHOUSE

For Vince Costello it was a sudden transition from twenty years in professional football as player and coach to restaurant owner, but it is one he has made with great success. When he left the Kansas City Chiefs, he knew he wanted to be his own boss. Back in Ohio when he played for the Cleveland Browns, he owned and operated a boy's summer camp for five years. That experience taught him about selling, people management, and food service, so Vince's plunge into the restaurant business was not totally foreign. Vince is on hand keeping an eye on quality control of everything from food preparation and cleanliness to having the napkins folded just right. "I keep a daily list of customer complaints and go over them every evening to follow up and correct the problem right then. Take care of the quality, and the dollars will take care of themselves."

The asymetrical design of Costello's suits the unusual exterior of alternating horizontal bands of rough cedar and narrow strips of copper. The interior features plants, trees, wood, and glass. Different elevations with small groupings of tables surrounded by low plantings give privacy to each area yet do not block the view of the overhead plants. The high ceiling and extensive use of glass lends a bright, sunny atmosphere to the restaurant in the daytime and an airiness by night light.

A varied menu including excellent prime rib, steaks, veal, and lamb is available daily. A wide selection of fish, with a fresh fish specialty every day, enlarges the selection. An artistically arranged, eye-appealing salad bar is one of the true highlights of dining at Costello's.

Live entertainment in the lounge has attracted devoted fans of each night's featured music. Saturday afternoon is reserved for Old Kansas City-style jazz jam sessions.

Vince's outgoing personality, energy, and good management have made Costello's Greenhouse a wonderful addition to Kansas City's eating establishments.

1414 West 85th Street
333-5470

CRAB RANGOON

1 pound cream cheese
½ cup minced scallions
  (approximately
  2 bunches)
1 cup salad crabmeat
1 teaspoon onion salt
½ teaspoon white pepper
¼ teaspoon lemon juice

⅛ teaspoon tabasco
  2" x 2" wonton wrappers
1 egg white, beaten
  Hot mustard (either
  buy prepared or mix
  equal parts dry mustard
  with water)
SWEET & SOUR SAUCE

1. Beat cream cheese and fold in other ingredients.
2. Place approximately ½ ounce in wonton and fold into square.
3. On last fold tack with egg white.
4. Cook in 325° fat until golden brown.
5. Serve with hot mustard or Sweet & Sour Sauce.

SWEET & SOUR SAUCE

1 cup pineapple juice
1 tablespoon white vinegar
1 tablespoon lemon juice
¼ cup brown sugar

2 tablespoons soy sauce
¼ cup corn starch
¼ teaspoon ginger

1. Combine all ingredients (except cornstarch and ginger) in medium saucepan and bring to boil. Thicken with corn starch.
2. Reduce heat and add ginger and simmer for 10 minutes.
3. Cool and serve.

COSTELLO'S GREENHOUSE

CAESAR SALAD

1 cup olive oil
1 cup red wine vinegar
2 tablespoons lemon juice
1½ teaspoon dry mustard
1½ teaspoon worcestershire
   sauce
7 coddled (2-minute) eggs

10 garlic cloves, minced
5 ounces anchovy fillets,
   minced
2 heads romaine, cored,
   separated, washed, and
   chilled
Parmesan Cheese, grated

1. Combine all ingredients except romaine and Parmesan cheese in plastic or wooden container. Make sure to scoop congealed whites from inside of eggshells.
2. Break romaine into bite-size pieces; place in wooden bowls and sprinkle with Parmesan cheese.
3. Add 8 to 10 ounces of dressing; stir well, then toss.
4. Serve on four chilled plates.

BOUILLABAISSE

2 cups fish stock
2 cups tomato juice
1 onion, minced
½ medium-size carrot,
   minced
2 ribs celery, minced
2 cloves garlic, minced
½–1 cup olive oil
½–1 cup flour
½ teaspoon onion salt
½ teaspoon white pepper

¼ teaspoon orange rind
⅛ teaspoon nutmeg
⅛ teaspoon saffron
2 tablespoons sherry
½ cup bay scallops
½ cup (26–30) shrimp,
   peeled and deveined
½ cup white fish (sole,
   snapper, flounder,
   etc.), diced

1. Combine fish stock and tomato juice and bring to a boil.
2. Place minced onion, carrots, celery, and garlic in hot olive oil and briefly sauté.
3. Add flour to make a light roux. Add minced vegetable mix to fish stock and simmer 20 minutes, then strain.
4. Add all spices, rubbing saffron between fingers while adding; simmer 10 minutes.
5. Add fish beginning with scallops, then shrimp, and finally fish; cook until tender. Serve in large dish.

NOTE: If desired garnish with a small lobster tail or steamed clam.

FRUIT FONDUE

Use 4 ounces each of any two or three kinds of fruit that are in season (canteloupe, honeydew, strawberries, or bananas). Dice or slice into bite-size pieces. Heat your favorite hot fudge and serve in fondue dish with fruit arranged on a plate. Dip fruit in hot fudge using fondue forks or skewers.

Dinner for Six

Chilled Mousse of Avocado with Bacon and Walnuts

Crisped Duck with Raspberry Sauce and Cashew Rice

String Beans and Shallots

Mixed Greens with Yoghurt Dressing

Deep Apple Custard Tart

Wines:

With appetizer—Dry Creek Fumé Blanc, 1981

With main course—Jordan Cabernet Sauvignon, 1978

Mark Prece, Chef

Bob Clark, Manager

Daniel Bendas, Director

CRYSTAL PAVILION

L ift your spirits on the darkest day with lunch or dinner at the Crystal Pavilion. No gloomy booths or stuffy candlelight here; the whole restaurant is light and airy. The supports for the clear glass walls and roof are painted a fresh white, highlighted with discreet pastels. The tables are pale, natural wood, and the chairs and benches are upholstered in a cheerful, flower-patterned chintz. Even the tiled floor was choosen to contribute to the fresh, light atmosphere.

We know you will enjoy the food. At lunchtime, you may choose to sit and watch an appetizing variety of omelettes being prepared. Lunch in the Pavilion is light, but satisfying. Try the spinach noodles, or the terrines, pates and relishes. The Crystal Pavilion is a perfect place at dinner to enjoy a sampler of appetizers—perhaps avocado, bacon crisps and walnuts. Then try Raspberry Duckling, or Lamb Chops with Garlic Cream. And leave room for a rich dessert from our own bakery.

2450 Grand   471-2003

CHILLED MOUSSE OF AVOCADO
WITH BACON AND WALNUTS

1½ cups fresh avocado pulp
4 teaspoons fresh-squeezed lemon juice
2 cups CRÈME FRAÎCHE
2 cups whipping cream
2 cups scallions, coarsely chopped
½ teaspoon thyme leaves, dried
1 teaspoon Kosher salt
¼ teaspoon cayenne pepper

2 teaspoons shallots, coarsely chopped
5½ teaspoons unflavored gelatin
1½ cups beef consommé Kosher salt
2 tablespoons walnuts, finely chopped
3 slices bacon, fried, crumbled

1. Puree the avocado pulp with the lemon juice until very smooth. Reserve.
2. Combine, in a saucepan, the Crème Fraîche, 1½ cups whipping cream, scallions, thyme, salt, cayenne, and shallots. Gently simmer until the liquid is reduced by half. Strain through cheese cloth and measure out 1 cup.
3. Dissolve 5 tablespoons of gelatin into the remaining ½ cup of cream and 1 cup of consommé. Add to the measured cream reduction and stir to blend. Fold in the pureed avocado.
4. Dissolve the remaining ½ teaspoon of gelatin into the remaining consommé. Adjust with salt until a reasonably salty flavor is obtained.
5. Lightly oil six 3½–4 ounce ramekins. Spoon the salted consommé evenly in each ramekin. Allow to chill completely in the refrigerator.
6. Fill each ramekin half full with the avocado cream puree.
7. Sprinkle the chopped walnuts evenly over the puree in each ramekin.

8. Fill the ramekins with the remaining puree.

9. Tightly cover the molds with plastic wrap and allow to chill completely, approximately 2 hours.

10. At the time of service, unmold each mousse onto service plates, sprinkle each with bacon and garnish, if desired, with neatly diced fresh vegetables, such as tomatoes, zucchini, red pepper, or green pepper around each mousse.

NOTE: We also serve this mousse as a fresh fruit salad accompaniment.

CRÈME FRAÎCHE

2 *cups whipping cream*
2 *tablespoons lemon juice,*
   freshly squeezed

½ *teaspoon salt*

Combine cream, lemon juice, and salt and stir to thoroughly blend. Cover tightly and allow to stand at room temperature for 24 hours.

CRISPED DUCK WITH RASPBERRY SAUCE AND CASHEW RICE

3 (4–6 pound) ducklings	RASPBERRY SAUCE
6 tablespoons SEASONED SALT	CASHEW RICE

1. Preheat oven to 350°.
2. Prepare the ducks by removing the wings at the first joint from the breast, removing the knuckles on the legs and trimming any excess skin and fat. Rub the entire outer surface and cavity of each duck with 2 tablespoons of the Seasoned Salt. Place the ducks in pans fitted with racks to allow for adequate draining.
3. Roast the ducks in oven for 1½–1¾ hours until the skin is crisp and the natural juices are clear. Remove and allow to cool completely on the racks. Raise oven temperature to 425°.
4. Halve the ducks, discarding the back bone. Remove all bones with the exception of the thigh, wing, and leg. Separate the leg from the breast of each half and reserve.
5. Before serving, reheat the ducks in oven for 6–8 minutes. Then crisp them for 10 seconds under the broiler. Serve with Raspberry Sauce and Cashew Rice.

SEASONED SALT

½ cup Kosher salt	1½ tablespoons rosemary, dried
1 tablespoon fresh garlic, finely minced	¾ teaspoon paprika
¾ teaspoon ground white pepper	¾ teaspoon thyme leaves, dried
¾ teaspoon oregano leaves, dried	¾ teaspoon poultry seasoning

Combine all ingredients in a mixing bowl and thoroughly blend. Reserve.

CRYSTAL PAVILION

RASPBERRY SAUCE

½ cup grenadine
½ cup fresh-squeezed
   orange juice
½ cup orange Curacao
1½ cups raspberry vinegar

¼ cup granulated sugar
Pinch Kosher salt
1 orange, zested by peeling
   and cutting into thin
   strips
2 tablespoons cornstarch

1. Combine, in a saucepan, the Grenadine, orange juice, Curacao, raspberry vinegar, sugar, salt, and *half* of the orange zest. Reserve the remaining zest for later use. Bring this mixture to a simmer and allow to simmer slowly for 15–18 minutes. Remove from heat and strain through cheesecloth.
2. Place the sauce in a clean saucepan, reserving ¼ cup. Dissolve the cornstarch in the reserved liquid. Bring the sauce to a boil and whip in the dissolved cornstarch. Reduce the heat and allow to simmer for 3 minutes.
3. While the sauce is simmering, finely sliver the remaining orange zest. Add to the sauce and simmer for 2 minutes more.
4. Remove the sauce from the heat, adjust the seasoning or sweetness level to your liking.

NOTE: *To zest an orange, peel with very sharp knife or potato peeler so that there is no white pith.*

CASHEW RICE

½ tablespoon butter, melted
½ medium-size onion,
    peeled, diced
½ cup converted white rice
1 cup chicken stock or broth

1 bay leaf
Table salt
Ground white pepper
½ cup cashews, roasted

1. Preheat oven to 400°.
2. Sauté the onions in the butter until transparent. Add the rice and stir to thoroughly coat with the butter.
3. Pour in the chicken broth, add the bay leaf, and bring the mixtures to a boil, stirring occasionally.
4. Cover the pan and place in a oven until the rice is tender and the liquid is absorbed.
5. Using a meat fork, stir in salt and pepper to taste. Serve the rice with the toasted cashews sprinkled over top.

STRING BEANS AND SHALLOTS

½ cup butter, softened
¼ cup shallots, minced
2 pounds fresh string beans,
    trimmed, blanched

½ cup chicken stock
Salt
Ground black pepper

1. Heat the butter in a sauté pan. Sauté the shallots in the butter until transparent, but not brown.
2. Add the beans and chicken stock and toss to blend all ingredients. Continue cooking until the beans are hot and the liquid is reduced to a glaze.
3. Adjust seasoning with salt and pepper and serve.

MIXED GREENS with YOGHURT DRESSING

1 head bibb lettuce
1 head romaine lettuce
½ head iceberg lettuce
1 large tomato, diced

3 hard-cooked eggs,
  coarsely chopped
½ cup bacon, diced and
  cooked, well-drained
  YOGHURT DRESSING

1. Trim the greens of all unusable leaves and remove the cores. Wash thoroughly and allow to drain well. Tear the lettuce by hand into bite-size pieces and toss to blend.
2. Mound the greens on chilled salad plates and garnish each with equal portions of tomato, chopped egg, and bacon. Serve with the dressing.

YOGHURT DRESSING

1 egg yolk
¾ cup vegetable oil
2 tablespoons red wine
  vinegar
¾ cup plain yoghurt
½ teaspoon table salt

½ teaspoon ground white
  pepper
2 tablespoons chopped fresh
  parsley
2 tablespoons fresh dill
2 tablespoons onion

1. Make a mayonnaise, using the egg yolk, oil, and vinegar. Fold in the yoghurt.
2. Add the salt, pepper, parsley, dill, and onion. Stir until well-blended. Chill before serving.

NOTE: As a variation add diced cucumber and minced garlic to the dressing according to your taste.

DEEP APPLE CUSTARD TART

1¾ cups flour
  1 cup butter, melted
2½ teaspoons baking powder
2½ cups granulated sugar
  4 eggs

1 pound baking apples,
     peeled and cored before
     weighing
½ teaspoon ground
     cinnamon

1. Preheat oven to 300°.
2. In the bowl of an electric mixer, combine the flour, ½ cup butter, baking powder, 1¼ cup sugar, and 2 eggs. Mix the ingredients until a smooth dough is formed. Press the dough into the bottom of an 8-inch by 3-inch springform pan.
3. Slice the apples into ½-inch-thick slices and press into the dough vertically. Sprinkle evenly with cinnamon.
4. Bake the tart for 1 hour.
5. Combine the remaining butter, sugar, and eggs in the bowl of the mixer and beat to incorporate all ingredients. Pour over the apples and continue baking for an additional 25–30 minutes. Remove and cool before unmolding.

NOTE: Other fresh fruits can be substituted for apples.

The
DINNER HORN
Country Inn

Dinner for Eight

Sweet Pickled Onion Rings

Cheese Bread Sticks

Spring Broccoli Soup

Chicken Bonnie

Oven-Baked Rice

Cheese Broiled Tomatoes

Golden Pumpkin Muffins

Dinner Horn Pie

Wine:

Robert Mondavi Fumé Blanc

Bonnie and Richard Kellenberg, Owners

DINNER HORN COUNTRY INN

The Dinner Horn Country Inn is Bonnie Kellenberg's dream come true. Cooking tasty food and sharing it with her friends has been a joy for Bonnie since her childhood on a farm in eastern Missouri. She majored in home economics at Iowa State University, taught in the Kansas City and Parkville school systems and catered for parties and weddings for ten years before building the Dinner Horn and her lovely Rose Garden. She now carries on her catering on a grand scale, from a simple cake and punch reception in the gardens of The Dinner Horn, to extravagant social catering at locations all over the city.

Bonnie's heart's desire was to open "Bonnie's Tea Room," but The Dinner Horn could hardly be called a tea room with its expansive façade, three large dining rooms, two with wood-burning fireplaces, and the Country Tavern. One feels like a guest in the Kellenbergs' home because of the coziness and warmth about the rooms and the style of service.

The restaurant is a new building in the Pennsylvania Dutch architectural tradition situated on a fifteen-acre wooded hilltop in Platte County, fifteen minutes north of downtown Kansas City. It has seating capacity of 240, including the banquet rooms downstairs. While the building is residential in character, it is constructed to commercial restaurant standards. The name "Dinner Horn" comes from an 1873 painting by Winslow Homer depicting the lady of the house standing on her porch blowing a trumpet-like horn calling her men in from the fields for lunch. A reproduction of the original painting was painted by Kansas City artist Jim Hamil and hangs in the entrance of the Inn.

Bonnie says, "Our dinner menu is based on the Pennsylvania Dutch tradition of seven sours and seven sweets. It takes about five courses to accomplish this. We have one price for each complete dinner because if people ordered à la carte they might not get the seven sours and seven sweets." The Dutch relish cupboard, where guests help themselves, provides at least four of those sour and sweet tastes. The salad, hot muffins and choice of nine or ten entrees, combined with dessert gives more than ample opportunity to complete the delicious task. The restaurant's original dinner service has expanded to include Sunday hours and weekday luncheon.

The Dinner Horn is family oriented and offers well-prepared, graciously served American specialties in generous portions. As Bonnie Kellenberg said, "No one comes to The Dinner Horn expecting to lose weight."

2820 N.W. Barry Road   436-8700

SWEET PICKLED ONION RINGS

½ cup sugar
½ cup red wine vinegar
1 teaspoon salt
   Red food coloring

½ teaspoon mustard seed
1¼ pounds onions, sliced
   and separated into rings
1 tablespoon grenadine

Mix sugar, vinegar, salt, food coloring, and mustard seed. Bring to a boil, then add onions and reduce heat to simmer. Cover and simmer for 3 minutes and then add the grenadine. Refrigerate.

This keeps for almost 2 weeks so it is ready for that extra touch to enhance any meal.

CHEESE BREAD STICKS

2 packages dry yeast
1½ cups warm water
2 tablespoons sugar
½ cup salad oil or olive oil
4-4½ cups flour

1 teaspoon salt
3 egg whites, slightly
   beaten
Coarse baker's salt
Grated Parmesan cheese

1. Preheat oven to 375°.
2. Add yeast to warm water and add sugar. Set aside until yeast mixture activates. Add oil. Slowly sift in flour and salt, mixing until you have a smooth dough.
3. Roll out pieces of dough the size of pencils and twist two together. Brush with egg whites and sprinkle with baker's salt and Parmesan cheese.
4. Bake on greased cookie sheet in oven for 20 minutes.

The recipe calls for either salad oil or olive but olive oil naturally gives the bread sticks a distinctive Italian flavor. Choose whichever suits your palate.

SPRING BROCCOLI SOUP

1 *bunch broccoli*
4 *tablespoons butter*
¾ *cup chopped onion*
2 *tablespoons flour*
2 *cups chicken broth*
1½ *teaspoons Worcestershire sauce*

1½ *teaspoons Tabasco sauce*
¾ *teaspoon salt*
2 *cups milk*
1 *cup grated sharp Cheddar cheese*
¼ *cup chopped fresh parsley*

1. Cut broccoli into tiny florets. Cook in salted water until tender. Drain.
2. Melt butter; add onions and sauté until tender.
3. Blend in flour and gradually add chicken broth, stirring all the while. Heat slowly until mixture boils. Add the Worcestershire sauce, Tabasco sauce, salt, broccoli, and milk. Sprinkle in grated cheese. Stir until melted.
4. Serve garnished with fresh parsley.

Fresh broccoli is absolutely essential for this recipe . . . frozen just does not have enough flavor.

Dinner for Four

Smoked Salmon Plate
Fresh Spinach Salad
Honeydew Sorbet
Roast Duckling with Cumberland Sauce
Fresh Raspberries with Kirsch Sabayon

Wines:
With the Salmon Plate—Deutz, Brut Champagne
With the Salad—St. Clement Sauvignon Blanc, 1981
With the Duck—Stags Leap Wine Cellars Cabernet Sauvignon
"Stags Leap Vineyards," 1979
With Raspberries—Chateau St. Jean Select Late Harvest
Johannisburg Riesling "Robert Young Vinegard," 1981

Cliff Bath, Owner
Joe Mercier, General Manager
Bob Palmgren, Chef

HARRY STARKER'S

Harry Starker's subtle, beveled-glass entry way is a hint of the aesthetics that will indeed impress you inside this restaurant. Once you enter the lobby, a spectacular beveled stained-glass dome, as well as the wide oval staircase, gently pull one's eye upward to the bar and cocktail lounge of this tri-level restaurant. While the entrance is of discreet traditional architecture, the rest of the restaurant, decorated with British artifacts, suggests a posh London tavern.

The menu, served with wholesome, friendly service, is varied with seafood, steaks, and specialties. Among the entrees are such items as Dover Sole, Rack of Lamb, Breast of Chicken Fromage, and Veal Limonata. The wine list of 135 wines (nurtured by Bob Bath, the restaurant's Assistant General Manager and nephew of its owner) is a satisfying complement to your meal.

Over the past eleven years, Harry Starker's has grown as a local favorite and, according to leading restaurant publications, is among America's top 75 single unit restaurants in its annual volume of business.

Owned and operated by Cliff Bath, with able assistance from General Manager Joe Mercier and Chef Bob Palmgren, Harry Starker's is a favorite place to spend an entire evening.

Bath named the restaurant after an old Englishman he happened on in a dictionary of biographical names. "I liked the ring to the name, Harry Starker," relates Bath, of English descent himself, slowly enunciating the syllables. "Plus, he was a jovial guy, known to consume large amounts of liquor and fine food. He rubbed shoulders with all sorts of people, rich and poor, and thus was a good model for my restaurant."

Bath learned his trade studying in the School of Hotel and Restaurant Administration at Oklahoma State and working nine years for Gilbert-Robinson. He opened Harry Starker's in 1972 and has gradually developed and enlarged the restaurant to its present stature.

Old Harry Starker would applaud Cliff Bath's style.

200 Nichols Road   753-3565

SMOKED SALMON PLATE

8 ounces smoked salmon, small dice

4 eggs, hard-cooked, yolk and white diced separately

1 red Bermuda onion, finely diced

16 capers

16 toast rounds or crackers

On each of four crystal plates, place 2 ounces of salmon in the center. Arrange diced egg yolk around salmon in a ring. Follow with diced egg white, then diced Bermuda onion. Place four capers on top of salmon. Serve with toast rounds or plain water crackers.

NOTE: When shopping for smoked salmon, you will find varying degrees of price and quality, depending on the waters from whence it came. For this recipe we suggest using Nova Scotia Smoked Salmon or the "ultimate," Scotch Smoked Salmon.

FRESH SPINACH SALAD

2 bunches fresh spinach
1 (8-ounce) can sliced
  waterchestnuts
½ pound mushrooms, sliced

2 eggs, hard-cooked, diced
2 slices bacon, fried,
  crumbled
CHUTNEY DRESSING
3 tablespoons cognac

1. On each of four salad plates, place one-fourth of the fresh chilled spinach leaves. Garnish each salad with sliced waterchestnuts, sliced fresh mushrooms, 1 tablespoon of diced hard-cooked egg, and 1 tablespoon of cooked crumbled bacon.
2. In copper sauté pan, heat 1 cup of Chutney Dressing until simmering. Lace dressing with cognac and bring to a slight boil. Ignite cognac and allow to flame. Immediately ladle over each salad and serve.

CHUTNEY DRESSING

1 (7.5-ounce) jar Major
  Grey Chutney
6 tablespoons Pommery
  mustard
1 clove garlic, crushed

1 tablespoon sugar
½ cup red wine vinegar
2 cups olive oil
1 cup water
Salt and pepper

In a blender, place chutney, mustard, garlic, and sugar and puree for 3 minutes or until a smooth paste has formed. Then add red wine vinegar until incorporated. Slowly add oil while blender is running until all is incorporated. Finish with water, salt and pepper to taste and place in clean container and refrigerate until ready for service.

HONEYDEW SORBET

1 medium-size honeydew,
   seeds and rind removed,
   cut into 2" pieces
Juice of ½ lemon

Pinch of Kosher salt
½ cup sugar
1½ cups water

Place honeydew and lemon juice in blender and puree. In a separate bowl place the salt, sugar, and water and whisk until dissolved. Pour sugar mixture in blender with honeydew and blend until all is incorporated. Place in ice cream machine and freeze according to manufacturer's instructions.

NOTE: If you do not have access to an ice cream freezer, you can instead place the mixture in the freezer section of your refrigerator until firm. Technically, you have made a fruit "ice," rather than a fruit "sorbet."

ROAST DUCKLING WITH CUMBERLAND SAUCE

2 (4½-pound) ducks
¼ cup Kosher salt
2 teaspoons white pepper
1 teaspoon paprika

1 teaspoon fennel seed
1 teaspoon whole thyme
 leaves
CUMBERLAND SAUCE

1. Preheat oven to 350°.
2. Cut off the wings at the second joint. Cut away all the duck fat from the cavities and excess fat from the neck.
3. Rub ducks with salt, pepper, paprika, fennel, and thyme.
4. Place a rack over a shallow roasting pan and fill with 2 quarts of water.
5. Place ducks on rack in roasting pan, breast side up. Do not let them touch each other. Roast in oven for 1½–2 hours.
6. When ducks are done, skin should be crisp and caramel color. Remove from oven and let rest for 10 minutes before serving. Serve with Cumberland Sauce.

CUMBERLAND SAUCE

½ cup fresh cranberries
1 teaspoon grated orange
 peel
1 large navel orange,
 peeled, seeded, and
 finely chopped
1 tablespoon brandy

½ cup port wine
¼ cup orange juice
¼ cup beef stock
1 teaspoon prepared
 mustard
Salt and pepper

1. In a stainless steel saucepan, place first five ingredients and heat until liquid has reduced by half. Then place remainder of ingredients in pan and bring to a boil. Reduce heat to a simmer, let simmer for 5 minutes and remove any scum that comes to the top.
2. Remove from stove and place in blender and puree until smooth. Salt and pepper to taste. Strain through fine sieve and serve.

FRESH RASPBERRIES WITH KIRSCH SABAYON

5 *egg yolks*	2 *ounces Kirschwasser*
1 *cup sugar*	2 *pints fresh raspberries*
1 *cup dry white wine*	*Fresh mint*

1. Beat egg yolks and sugar in copper or glass (not stainless steel) bowl with wire whisk until mixture is light-colored and forms a ribbon when whisk is lifted. Gradually beat in wine and kirschwasser, 1 tablespoon at a time.
2. Place bowl over saucepan of simmering water. Cook over low heat, whisking constantly until mixture thickens into fluffy custard, about 5 minutes. Immediately remove from heat.
3. Divide raspberries among four dessert dishes. Spoon Sabayon over berries; garnish with fresh mint sprigs and serve immediately.

NOTE: Be sure not to let the egg yolks curdle from overcooking. While the use of a hand whisk requires a little extra work, the effort is well worth the delicate light flavor you create.

HOULIHAN'S®
old place

Dinner for Four

Mushroom Escargot

Salad Houlihan

Stuffed Chicken Breast with Dill Butter Sauce

Apple Strudel Pie

Wine:

Robert Mondavi Chardonnay

Christian Brothers Zinfandel

Gilbert/Robinson, Inc., Owners

Mike McCarthy, Manager

John E. Cuff, Chef

HOULIHAN'S OLD PLACE

T om Houlihan had a men's clothing store on the Country Club Plaza for many years. It was only natural, when remodeling for the new restaurant got underway, that the delivery description for all the lumber, furniture, carpeting, and equipment was "It goes to Houlihan's old place." Thus this restaurant with its novel menu and decor got its name.

Houlihan's Old Place is the brainchild of Gilbert/Robinson, Inc., which is the out-growth of a partnership of Kansas City restaurateurs Joe and Bill Gilbert and Paul Robinson. Nationally recognized, Paul Robinson is the recipient of numerous awards including the Ivy Award and several Outstanding Interiors awards from Institutions.

Wood-inlaid walls and table tops, fabric ceilings, and lush greenery create a natural, relaxed setting complemented by one-of-a-kind artifacts including Tiffany lamps, brass accents, stained glass, English pub mirrors, and antique advertising art and posters. Equally unusual is Houlihan's imaginative menu, offering everything from salads, sandwiches, burgers, and steaks to escargots, roast duck, and seafood. In keeping with the trend toward natural and nutritious foods, all items are prepared with the freshest ingredients available and light sauces, if any.

"Houlihan's Old Place was an attempt to put together a coming new life style—a more informal style of living and eating. At a time (1972) when the industry trend was toward a limited menu, we went the opposite direction. We anticipated a market trend with our eclectic menu that appeals to appetites at 4 p.m., the dinner hour, or 10:30 p.m."

Houlihan's bar and lounge are traditionally popular social spots. A loyal entourage is attracted by the bartenders' potent beverages as well as by an interesting assortment of specialty drinks such as the famous Houlihan's Cappuccino.

The restaurant has been one of Kansas City's top dining establishments for over 11 years, a fact recently verified when Houlihan's made the Top 10 list for the 1982 Silver Spoon Awards, presented by *Corporate Report* magazine.

4743 Pennsylvania   561-3141

MUSHROOM ESCARGOT

16 large fresh mushroom caps (about the size of a silver dollar)

32 teaspoons soft ESCARGOT BUTTER

16 extra-large whole escargots

½ cup bread crumbs

16 bacon squares, 1" pieces

1. Preheat oven to 450°.
2. Remove the stems from the caps of the mushrooms (reserve them for another use) and place the mushrooms, cap side down, in an oven-proof dish.
3. Spoon a teaspoon of Escargot Butter into each mushroom cap.
4. Place a whole escargot onto the butter pressing lightly into the cap.
5. Place an additional teaspoon of Escargot Butter onto the snail itself.
6. Coat the top of each mushroom with bread crumbs.
7. Place 1 bacon square on top of each mushroom and bake in pre-heated oven until the bacon is golden brown and slightly crisp.
8. Divide into serving dishes and pour the butter remaining in the baking dish over each portion.

ESCARGOT BUTTER

½ pound butter, room temperature

3 tablespoons minced parsley

2 tablespoons finely minced onion

1 teaspoon black pepper

1½ tablespoons fresh minced garlic

1 tablespoon fresh lemon juice

Combine butter with parsley and onion. Add seasonings and blend until well incorporated.

SALAD HOULIHAN

1 pound mixed salad
  greens (a combination
  of Iceberg, Romaine, and
  Chicory)
½ cup shredded red cabbage
1 tomato, cored and cut into
  8 small wedges

2 bacon strips, cooked crisp
  and broken into bite-size
  pieces
½ cup cheddar cheese
½ cup herb and garlic
  croutons
  COUNTRY CLUB
  DRESSING

Arrange salad greens in attractive serving bowl and top with tomato, bacon, cheese, and Croutons. Serve with Country Club Dresing.

COUNTRY CLUB DRESSING

1 teaspoon salt
½ teaspoon white pepper
2 tablespoons sugar
2 tablespoons paprika

¼ cup white wine vinegar
1 cup salad oil
4 ounces blue cheese,
  crumbled

Dissolve seasonings in vinegar, and combine with oil; mix vigorously. Add blue cheese and chill before serving.

STUFFED CHICKEN BREASTS with DILL BUTTER SAUCE

8 (6-ounce) boneless
   chicken breasts, skinned
8 ounces herb & garlic
   cheese (Alouette or
   Boursin Brand)
   SEASONED FLOUR

EGG WASH
2 cups fresh white
   breadcrumbs
½ cup clarified butter
1 bunch watercress
   DILL BUTTER SAUCE

1. Preheat oven to 375°.
2. Place the breast in between sheets of waxed paper, and flatten with the broad side of a large knife, or a meat mallet to a thickness of ¼ inch.
3. To stuff the breasts, lay each breast on a work surface with the skin side *down*. Place 2 tablespoons of the cheese in the center of the breasts. Carefully fold the sides of the chicken over the breast, covering the cheese completely. Reshape chicken breasts by squeezing the ends together. Cover the stuffed breasts with plastic wrap and chill at least one hour.
4. After chilling the breasts, dredge lightly in the seasoned flour, coating evenly on all sides. Shake off any excess flour. Dip the flour-dusted breasts in the Egg Wash, coating the breasts evenly with the wash. Drain well before continuing. Coat the washed breasts with the fresh crumbs, shaking off any excess.
5. Place a large sauté pan on medium heat. Place ¼ cup butter in the pan and heat until just hot. Place the breaded breasts in the pan and sauté until the first side is golden brown. Carefully turn the breasts over. Immediately place the skillet in oven and bake until second side is golden brown (about 8–10 minutes).
6. Remove the breasts from the pan, drain well to remove all excess fat and place on a serving platter.
7. Garnish the platter with watercress and ladle two ounces of Dill Butter Sauce over the tops of the breast.

SEASONED FLOUR

1 cup flour
2 tablespoons 'Aromat'
   Seasoning (Yellow
   Label)

1 tablespoon 'Lawry's'
   Seasoning Salt
1 tablespoon ground white
   pepper

In a small mixing bowl, thoroughly combine the flour and seasonings. Mix well with your hands to insure an even distribution of the seasonings.

EGG WASH

4 eggs, fresh

3 tablespoons salad oil

In a small bowl, whisk together the eggs and oil. Use a hand whip for best results. Whisk rapidly to insure complete blending.

DILL BUTTER SAUCE

1 tablespoon minced shallots	¼ teaspoon Tabasco sauce
¾ cup dry white wine	¾ teaspoon 'Lawry's' Seasoning Salt
1 cup heavy whipping cream	1½ tablespoon lemon juice
½ teaspoon Worcestershire sauce	1½ teaspoons dill weed, preferably fresh
	1 pound unsalted butter

1. Combine the minced shallots and wine in a medium-size saucepan. Place the pan over medium heat, and allow the mixture to reduce to two tablespoons.
2. After the reduction is complete, add the cream, stirring well. Allow the cream to come up to the simmering point before continuing.
3. Add the remaining ingredients except the butter to the simmering cream mixture. Allow the sauce base to simmer, stirring often until it has reduced to one-half cup, and is slightly thickened.
4. Cut the butter into pieces the size of a walnut. Lower the heat under the sauce to just barely simmering. Using a hand whip, whisk in the butter, three pieces at a time. DO NOT allow the sauce to boil while adding the butter. Whisk constantly while adding the butter until all has been added. When the butter addition is complete, remove the sauce from the range and hold warm until needed. DO NOT allow the sauce to boil after the butter has been added.

HOULIHAN'S OLD PLACE

APPLE STRUDEL PIE

6 cups apples, peeled, sliced
  ¼" thick
1¼ cups sugar, granulated
¼ cup brown sugar, light
1 tablespoon flour
¼ cup dark currants
  Juice of ½ lemon
1 teaspoon cinnamon

½ teaspoon nutmeg
1 tablespoon butter, melted
2 tablespoons cold water
1 (10") unbaked PIE SHELL
  STRUDEL CRUMB
    TOPPING
  STRUDEL GLAZE

1. Preheat oven to 425°.
2. Place the sliced apples in a large mixing bowl and add the sugars, flour, currants, lemon juice, and seasonings to the apples and toss to evenly distribute. Add the melted butter and water and toss to moisten.
3. Neatly, pile the apple mix into the unbaked shell. Pile, *without packing*, the Strudel Crumb Topping on the pie, completely covering the entire surface. Place in oven and bake 10 minutes. Reduce heat to 325° and bake 1 hour. Remove from oven and cool to warm.
4. While warm, drizzle the Strudel Glaze over the pie. Cool completely before serving.

HOULIHAN'S OLD PLACE

PIE SHELL

3 ounces cream cheese, soft
8 tablespoons margarine,
   softened

1 cup flour

1. In a mixing bowl, cream the cheese and margarine together until light and creamy. Add flour and beat until smooth. Chill before using.
2. Flour work surface lightly. Place dough on floured surface and dust top of dough with flour. Roll out to 10½ inches diameter and ⅛ inch thickness.
3. Place into a 10-inch pie tin and insure that there are no air pockets between the dough and side of tin. Trim excessive dough away and crimp sides.

STRUDEL CRUMB TOPPING

⅔ cup flour
¼ cup butter, soft
¼ cup sugar

¼ cup brown sugar
½ teaspoon cinnamon
¼ teaspoon ground nutmeg

Cut the butter into the flour with two knives until mixture is crumbly. Gently mix in the sugars and spices. Use immediately as a pie topping.

STRUDEL GLAZE

1 cup powdered sugar

2 tablespoons lemon juice,
   fresh, strained

In a small bowl, mix the powdered sugar and lemon juice and mix smooth. Cover with plastic wrap until needed.

Dinner for Four

Fettucine all' Alfredo

Tomato, Onion, and Anchovy Salad

Vitelli Veronese

Brandy Alexander Mousse

Café Calypso

Wines:

With Fettucine—DeSimone Castel Vetrano Bianco

With Vitelli Veronese—Tavel Rose or Pinot Grigio

Jasper Mirabile, Owner

JASPER'S

Almost thirty years ago Jasper's was a tiny mom-and-pop operation. In 1953 Jasper Mirabile and his father bought Rose's Tavern, a small dingy neighborhood watering hole. They continued to serve drinks, but in addition Jasper's mother—long before the health laws prohibited it—would cook at home Southern Italian dishes redolent with garlicky tomato sauces and then bring them steaming to the bar. There, customers would eat with relish Mama Mirabile's home-cooked fare.

The restaurant is still a family operation. But now Jasper's has a new bar and three lavishly baroque dining rooms, distinguished by tables covered with pink tablecloths and plush scarlet chairs and banquettes. Jasper's mother had attracted such a following that soon the Mirabiles built a kitchen on the spot for her and subsequently hired a full-time chef. Business has not waned for twenty-seven years, and the Mirabiles attribute their success to family ownership and a meticulous concern for details.

In Roman splendor, the restaurant now serves Northern Italian food, which employs ample quantities of heavy cream, cheese, and butter. "Bere, Mangiare Bene—Eat and Drink Well," the restaurant's motto urges, and at Jasper's you'll do both.

405 West 75th Street   363-3003

VITELLI VERONESE

1 pound veal scallops,
   pounded thin
½ cup bread crumbs
¼ cup Parmesan cheese

Rind of 2 lemons, grated
3 eggs, beaten
½ cup butter
½ cup olive oil

Dredge veal in flour. Shake off excess. In a large bowl mix bread crumbs, cheese, and lemon rind. Dip veal in eggs, then in bread crumb mixture. In a large skillet, melt ½ cup butter with ½ cup olive oil. Place veal in pan when oil/butter is hot. Fry on both sides until golden brown. Serve immediately garnished with lemon slices. Salt and pepper to taste.

NOTE: The veal used for this recipe is from the leg.

BRANDY ALEXANDER MOUSSE

6 ounces semi-sweet
  chocolate bits
1 tablespoon instant coffee
1½ tablespoons cold water
4 egg yolks
1½ tablespoons brandy

1½ tablespoons crème de
  cacao
4 egg whites
½ cup heavy cream, whipped
2 teaspoons sugar
2 teaspoons ground
  almonds
2 teaspoons Kahlua

1. In the top of a double boiler, melt the chocolate bits. Add the coffee mixed with the water, stirring until the mixture forms a smooth paste.
2. Beat the egg yolks until they are a pale lemon color. Add to the chocolate mixture and stir until well blended.
3. Add the brandy and crème de cacao and stir until the mixture begins to thicken. Pour into the bowl and let the mixture cool.
4. Beat the egg whites until stiff and fold carefully but completely into the cooled chocolate mixture.
5. Put the mixture into a pastry bag fitted with a medium-size fluted tip. Pipe the mixture into four stemmed dessert glasses or into pretty cocktail glasses. Chill thoroughly in the refrigerator for several hours.
6. For the topping, whip the cream until thick. Add the sugar, almonds, and Kahlua. Continue whipping the cream until stiff enough to hold its shape. Spoon the cream over the mousse just before serving.

CAFE CALYPSO

1 ounce Korbel brandy
4 ounces Kahlua
2 cups hot coffee

4 tablespoons whipped cream

In each of four (6-ounce) heat-tempered goblets, put a splash of brandy, 1 ounce of Kahlua, and ½ cup hot coffee. Top with a tablespoon of whipped cream.

La Méditérranée

Dinner for Four

Escargots Gourmands

Salade de Saison

Mignon de Veau Polignac

Crème de Celeri

Mousse au Chocolat Blanc

Wines:

With Escargots—White Quincy, 1976

With Veal—Château Cos d'Estournel Bourdeaux Rouge, 1972

With Mousse—Moët et Chandon Champagne

Gilbert Jahier, Owner and Chef

For Gilbert Jahier, owner and chef of La Méditérranée, cooking runs in the family. His father is a chef in Orleans, France, where Gilbert grew up. His father feared that if Gilbert learned to cook at his knee the boy would be receiving special attention, so at age fifteen Gilbert was apprenticed to another restaurant. He worked there for three years.

Looking for better opportunities than those existing in France, Gilbert immigrated to this country at age twenty-three. He settled in Washington, D.C., and worked in such famous restaurants as Sans Souci and La Rive Gauche. Four years ago, in a move toward independence, he purchased a restaurant on Kansas City's Country Club Plaza. Here, in a fashion more typical of France than of the United States, he does the cooking while his gracious wife oversees the dining rooms.

The husband-wife combination complements the provincial flavor of the dining rooms. "We have tried to create a rustic-type restaurant here," says Gilbert, "—something like you'd see outside Paris. The paintings and the dominant use of the color red give the effect." It could easily be a restaurant in Orleans. Like father, like son.

4742 Pennsylvania

La Méditérranée

ESCARGOTS GOURMANDS

24 canned snails
2–3 tablespoons butter
     Pinch of minced shallot
1 tablespoon Cognac

2 tablespoons finely
   chopped tomato
1½ cups heavy cream
    Salt and pepper
    Croutons

1. Sauté snails 4 to 5 minutes in butter and add a pinch of minced shallot.
2. Deglaze with Cognac and add tomato.
3. Add heavy cream and stir until well blended.
4. Season to taste and simmer for 5 to 7 minutes or until sauce has thickened enough to coat a spoon.
5. Serve with croutons.

NOTE: This is optional, but you can improve the flavor of the snails by simmering them for 10 minutes before the above preparation. Place the snails in a saucepan, cover them with wine and add ¼ teaspoon each of thyme and basil and ½ of a small bay leaf. Don't let them boil or they'll get tough.

SALADE DE SAISON

1 *head of romaine, the outer leaves discarded, the remainder cleaned and torn into bite-size pieces*

8 *mushrooms, cleaned and thinly sliced*
2 *tomatoes, sliced*
  VINAIGRETTE
¼ *cup chopped parsley (approximately)*

1. Divide the lettuce among individual plates.
2. Place the mushrooms and tomatoes on top.
3. Before serving, pour on Vinaigrette and sprinkle parsley on top of each salad.

VINAIGRETTE

3 *tablespoons Jerez vinegar*
½ *teaspon Dijon mustard*
1½ *teaspoons chopped green pepper*
1½ *teaspoons chopped pimiento*

1 *teaspoon fresh tarragon, or ½ teaspoon dried tarragon*
  Pinch of minced garlic
  Pinch of minced shallots
⅔ *cup walnut oil*
  Salt and pepper

1. Mix the vinegar with the mustard.
2. Add the green pepper, pimiento, tarragon, garlic, and shallots and mix well.
3. Add the oil and season with salt and pepper to taste.

Walnut oil is not commonly used for salad dressings here in the United States, but it gives a distinctive and intriguing flavor.

MIGNON DE VEAU POLIGNAC

4 (8-ounce) mignons of veal
   (a mignon is a 1"-thick
   loin chop, boned)
   Salt and pepper
3 tablespoons butter

1 tablespoon minced shallot
¼ cup Porto wine
1 cup DEMI-GLACE de
   VIANDE
2 ounces raisins

1. Season the meat with salt and pepper.
2. Brown each side quickly in 2 tablespoons butter. Reduce heat and sauté for 7 minutes on each side. Remove from pan and keep warm in a 200° oven.
3. Add minced shallot to the pan and deglaze with Porto wine. Simmer until reduced by half.
4. Add Demi-Glace de Viande and simmer 5 minutes.
5. Add raisins and remaining butter. Taste for seasoning and adjust if necessary.
6. To serve, pour the sauce over the veal.

DEMI-GLACE de VIANDE

2 pounds veal bones
2 carrots, coarsely chopped
1 onion, coarsely chopped
2 stalks celery, coarsely
   chopped
2 tomatoes, coarsely
   chopped

½ cup white wine
1 tablespoon basil
2 teaspoons thyme
1 bay leaf
2 teaspoons salt
   Pepper to taste

1. Brown bones with vegetables and seasonings in a 450° oven.
2. When browned, add to stock pot. Cover with water and add the wine and seasonings.
3. Simmer 5 to 6 hours. Strain. (You should have about 5 quarts.)
4. Reduce 5 quarts to 1 quart, skimming from time to time. Adjust seasoning.

LA MÉDITÉRRANÉE

CRÈME DE CELERI

1 celery root, peeled
2 potatoes, peeled
1 medium onion

Salt and pepper
1 teaspoon nutmeg
2 to 3½ cups milk

1. Preheat oven to 400°.
2. Quarter celery root, potatoes, and onion. Arrange to fit tightly in a casserole.
3. Add salt, pepper, and nutmeg and cover with milk.
4. Bring the milk to a full boil and immediately remove from heat.
5. Cover casserole and cook in preheated oven for 35 minutes.
6. Pass through a blender until smooth textured. Adjust the seasonings.

The celery root, while common in France, is not too well known here. It has a spicy, peppery taste and goes especially well with game. You can obtain it here at some groceries.

MOUSSE AU CHOCOLAT BLANC

4 *ounces white chocolate*	½ *cup sugar*
1½ *tablespoons water*	1 *pint heavy cream*
2 *egg yolks*	*Dash of Kirsch*

1. Melt the chocolate with the water in a double boiler.
2. Combine egg yolks and sugar and slowly add chocolate mixture.
3. Beat the heavy cream until stiff and fold into the chocolate mixture.
4. Add a dash of Kirsch. Refrigerate before serving.

Chocolate mousse made with black chocolate is everywhere. Mousse made with white chocolate is unusual. The taste is different, much lighter.

nabil's

Dinner for Four

Escargot on Artichoke Bottoms

Carrot Pureé

Fillet with Brown Sauce and Heart of Palm

Romaine Salad with Mint Vinaigrette Dressing

Broadway Creme Caramel

Wines:

With Escargot—Dry Creek Fumé Blanc

With Fillet—Sterling Vineyards Cabernet Sauvignon

With Creme Caramel—Armagnac

Nabil Saleh, Owner

David Shapiro, Manager

"**It** was a logical progression to European cooking," Nabil Saleh casually recounts of the opening of Nabil's on Broadway. The 30-year-old restaurateur with a master's degree in Middle Eastern Studies had previously worked on Wall Street. What could make more sense?

Actually, the pieces do fit together. Dissatisfied with New York, Nabil returned to Kansas City where he had lived since he was seven years old, his parents having immigrated there from Lebanon. Nabil had learned to cook in New York from a circle of culinary-minded friends. So, in 1973, after his return from New York, Nabil opened Nabil's on Broadway, serving Middle Eastern food. "I did not have any confidence that it would go over," remembers Nabil, "I hoped a small, foreign restaurant would get a portion of the non-steak-and-potatoes crowd."

Nabil's on Broadway, now celebrating it's tenth year, continues to offer the finest in quality dining and service. The recipes are gathered from travels, so that every night the menu changes. The small, intimate dining room, newly decorated in simple but classic decor, adds to the complete dining experience.

Nabil's on Broadway is no longer Kansas City's best kept secret; but it is still a discovery.

3605 Broadway   531-0700

ESCARGOT ON ARTICHOKE BOTTOMS

8 artichoke bottoms	½ teaspoon white pepper
¾ cup butter	1 package frozen spinach
2 teaspoons garlic powder	8 canned snails

1. Preheat oven to 300°.
2. Heat artichoke bottoms in hot water. Drain.
3. Melt butter, garlic powder, pepper in roasting pan. Add spinach and snails to butter mixture. Bake 30 minutes.
4. Place spinach mixture on bottom of plate with artichoke bottom. Place snails on top of artichokes. Serve hot with lemon wedge.

NOTE: There are fresh and canned artichoke bottoms—canned are easier.

CARROT PUREÉ

1½ pounds baby carrots, cleaned and peeled	Milled white pepper to taste
2 tablespoons unsalted butter	

1. Cook carrots in lightly salted water until tender.
2. Pureé the carrots with the butter and pepper.
3. Serve aside beef on top of watercress bed.

NOTE: This dish may be prepared 2 hours ahead of time, then reheated in oven and piped through pastry bag.

FILLET WITH BROWN SAUCE AND HEART OF PALM

1 shallot, finely chopped
6 tablespoons butter
4 (8-ounce) beef fillets
6 ounces BROWN SAUCE

2 hearts of palm, sliced
  lengthwise
Dijon mustard (optional)
Paprika

1. Brown shallots in butter. Then sauté fillets in butter and shallots.
2. In another pan, heat Brown Sauce with hearts of palm.
3. To serve, place 1 beef fillet on each dinner plate and coat in sauce. Place heart of palm on top of beef. Top the heart of palm with a dollop of Dijon and dash of paprika.

This beef is a dramatic presentation and looks best on a plate not heavily garnished.

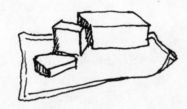

The Old Apple Farm

Dinner for Six

Mulled Cider

Apple, Grape, and Banana Salad

Baked Brisket of Beef
with Horseradish Sauce

Green Rice

Skillet Bread

Apple Crisp

Wine:

With Beef—Robert Mondavi Cabernet Sauvignon

Les and Lloyd Stephenson, Owners

Charlie Myers, Chef

"**Go** east, diners of Kansas City. Go east." This must have been the slogan of Les and Lloyd Stephenson in the early years of their thirty-seven-year-old restaurant. Located practically in Independence, on their family apple orchard well east of downtown Kansas City, the twin brothers felt they had to create a special restaurant to lure the hungry so far away from their home.

"We had a terrible location," declares Lloyd. "There was no local business when we opened so we had to survive on town traffic. The only way, as we saw it, to get people to drive this far was to have something outstanding. The food had to be different and had to have value." In keeping with their semi-rural setting, they devised an American menu with several apple and hickory-smoked items, oven-fresh rolls, and fried apple fritters. Inside, they created a home-like setting that is quaint, rustic, and charming.

In particular, the Stephensons oriented their restaurant to please women. "The woman decides where to go eat," says Lloyd. "She's got to like it. We've got to romance the women." To that end the brothers designed one of the first atmosphere restaurants in town.

The success of their first restaurant and family growth prompted the twins to open two more, one near Kansas City International Airport, the other in Jane, Missouri, near Bella Vista, Arkansas. Unfortunately, the Jane, Missouri, restaurant burned, but it should be open for business by publication of this book. Now Kansas City diners who want to sample some good American cooking can go east, or they can go north, or they can go south—it doesn't matter to the twins.

16401 East 40 Highway   373-5400
(5 miles east of Sports Complex)

SKILLET BREAD

2 cups flour
2½ teaspoons baking powder
1 teaspoon salt
½ teaspoon baking soda

1½ cups buttermilk
1 tablespoon butter
1 tablespoon peanut oil

1. Combine flour, baking powder, salt, and baking soda in a bowl. Stir buttermilk into dry ingredients.
2. Heat butter and oil in a 12-inch skillet. Pour batter into hot skillet. Cover and cook over low heat for 10–12 minutes.
3. Turn bread adding 1 tablespoon more butter to skillet. Cook it for 10 to 12 minutes more. Cut into wedges and serve.

Have lots of butter and preserves on the table for this treat. In the days of cooking over an open fire, this was known as "spider bread" because the skillets had legs that made them look like a spider hovering over the fire.

APPLE CRISP

8–9 medium-size apples,
    peeled, cored, and sliced
1¾ teaspoons cinnamon
2 cups sugar
1 cup + 2 tablespoons flour

2 tablespoons butter
1 teaspoon baking powder
½ teaspoon salt
1 egg

1. Preheat oven to 350°.
2. Blend apples with ½ of the cinnamon, ½ of the sugar, and 2 tablespoons of the flour.
3. Butter a baking dish with 1 tablespoon of butter. Place apple mix in dish and dot with the remaining butter.
4. In another bowl mix the rest of the sugar with the rest of the flour, cinnamon, baking powder, salt, and the egg. Mix until crumbly.
5. Sprinkle over apples and bake until brown and bubbly.
6. Serve warm with whipped cream or vanilla ice cream.

The Peppercorn Duck Club

Dinner for Four

Brie and Escargot

Peach Sorbet

Rack of Lamb

Anna Potatoes

Sautéed Snow Peas

Chocolate Pecan Pie

Wines:

With Brie and Escargot, Robert Mondavi Fumé Blanc

With Rack of Lamb, Chateau Brane—Cantenac Margaux '76

Phil Guttendorf, Chef

George Vizer, Food & Beverage Director

THE PEPPERCORN DUCK CLUB

One of Kansas City's favorite restaurants is The Peppercorn Duck Club. The ambiance is created by a comfortably elegant room of polished brass and plush surroundings. The specialty is rotisserie duckling, plump and crisp, accompanied by a variety of delicate sauces. Duck hunters are allowed to make advance arrangements for their bird to be expertly prepared in the Hyatt tradition for their dining pleasure in the Duck Club. Although duckling is the specialty, everything on the menu is a gourmet's delight. To accompany your meal the Market Island offers a splendid selection of fresh, colorful salads and pâté. And for dessert—The Ultra Chocolate bar will satisfy the sweetest tooth. Dozens of sumptuous chocolate items prepared in the pastry shop daily include chocolate chip pecan pie, double moist brownies, and mousses just to name a few. Truly a chocolate lover's paradise! The service is unmatched, making The Peppercorn Duck Club a remarkable dining experience.

2345 McGee Street   421-1234

BRIE AND ESCARGOT

2 (8-ounce) brie, split in half lengthwise	10 (6" round) filo sheets
8 snails	2 tablespoons butter, melted

1. Take split brie and with a small cutter, cut out four holes in each brie just large enough for the snails to fit in. Place snails in holes. Wrap brie and snails in the filo sheets, making sure the cheese is completely encased. Brush with melted butter and freeze.
2. Preheat oven to 400°.
3. Bake brie until the filo is golden brown. Let stand 10 minutes before cutting.

PEACH SORBET

32 ounces frozen peaches	1 bottle champagne
Juice of ⅓ lemon	2 cups peach liqueur
1¼ cup sugar	

Thaw peaches and pureé in blender or food processor. Combine all ingredients and mix well. Freeze hard. Run mix through a mixer or food processor. Refreeze until needed.

RACK OF LAMB

1½ cup fine diced onion
3 tablespoons fine diced
    garlic
1 cup olive oil
3 chopped fresh herbs
    (thyme, basil, tarragon,
    oregano, etc.)

1 (8-bone) rack of lamb,
    trimmed and frenched
    (ask butcher to do this
    for you)

1. Combine onion, garlic, olive oil, and herbs. Completely cover the rack of lamb with the mixture. Marinate for 48 hours. (This marinade will tenderize and flavor and help cut the strong lamb taste.)
2. Preheat oven to 375°.
3. Sear lamb in a hot skillet. Bake in oven until done as desired. Allow to set 10 minutes before slicing.

ANNA POTATOES

4 potatoes, sliced ¼" thick

Salt and pepper
8 tablespoons butter

1. Preheat oven to 375°.
2. Butter individual ovenproof molds or one large oven-proof mold. Arrange sliced potatoes in layers. Season each layer and dot with butter. Bake for 50 minutes or until done.

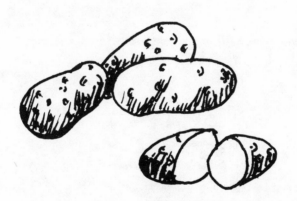

SAUTÉED SNOW PEAS

1 *pound snow peas*   *Salt and pepper*
2 *tablespoons butter*

Trim ends of snow peas. Heat a small amount of butter in sauté pan. Sauté snow peas for 2–3 minutes. Season with salt and pepper.

NOTE: For an oriental flair, sauté the snow peas in sesame oil and add a small amount of soy sauce.

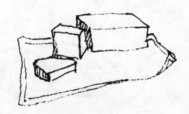

CHOCOLATE PECAN PIE

2 cups corn syrup
¼ cup flour
2½ tablespoons sugar
6 ounces sweet chocolate
   melted (Nestles morsels).

5 eggs, beaten
3 tablespoons melted butter
1 teaspoon vanilla
1 teaspoon salt
1 (10") pie shell, baked
   Pecan halves to cover
3 ounces chocolate chips

1. Preheat oven to 350°.
2. Mix corn syrup, flour, sugar, chocolate. Beat in eggs, add butter, vanilla, and salt. Fill pie shell and top with pecans. Bake for 35 minutes or until filling is set.
3. Decorate with chocolate chips and serve.

Dinner for Four

Champignons Magique

Steak Soup Plaza III

Roasted Rack of Lamb

Stir-fry Panache

Chocolatissimo

Wines:

With Champignons, Pouilly-Fumé, Le Fort, 1978

With Lamb, Robert Mondavi Chardonnay, 1978

Gilbert/Robinson, Inc., Owners

Larry Ziegler, Manager

Steve Ellenberg, Chef

PLAZA III

T he casually elegant, English atmosphere of Plaza III lends itself to relaxed dining. There are oriental rugs on parquet floors and hanging or potted plants all around. The restaurant is divided into separate rooms, each with a slightly varied atmosphere, but generally the restaurant is warmly lit and quiet. In most of the rooms, large oil paintings hang on rosy brick walls. The table linens are pink and the flowers are in shades of burgundy, rose, and pink, giving the entire restaurant a rosy hue. Plaza III is sophisticated but not stuffy or formal.

The food at Plaza III is Continental but not complicated. The luncheon menu offers salads, hearty sandwiches, seafood crepes, fresh vegetable omelets, and specialty items. Dinner emphasizes a selection of Continental delicacies as well as roast duck, steaks, and seafood. The wine list is extensive, and the service is attentive but not obtrusive.

Plaza III has won two Outstanding Interiors awards from *Institutions* and was voted one of the top restaurants in the country by *Sales and Marketing Management*. The restaurant also received the Number 1 ranking in the 1982 Silver Spoon Awards, which is presented annually by *Corporate Report* magazine of Kansas City (based on its readers' preference in dining establishments).

4749 Pennsylvania   756-0000

CHAMPIGNONS MAGIQUE

6 tablespoons butter
½ cup minced onion
½ cup minced celery
¾ teaspoon salt
¾ teaspoon pepper
¾ teaspoon thyme
¼ teaspoon dried rosemary
    leaves

¼ pound plus 12 (1") pieces
    Alaskan King Crab
    meat
1 ounce dry white wine
2 cups dry bread crumbs
12 fresh, large 'silver-
    dollar-size'
    mushroom caps
    CHEDDAR CHEESE
    SAUCE

1. Preheat oven to 350°.
2. Place the butter in a large skillet and allow to melt without browning. Add the vegetables and sauté until the onions are transparent.
3. When vegetables are tender, add the seasonings and ¼ pound crab meat. Allow to heat and add the wine and bread crumbs. Remove from heat and stir well. Allow to cool completely.
4. When the stuffing is cold, divide equally among the mushroom caps. Place the stuffed mushroom caps on a buttered baking sheet.
5. Place 1 piece of crab meat on top of the stuffing of each mushroom cap. Bake in preheated oven until hot and golden brown.
6. To serve, place three stuffed caps on each plate. Mask with Cheddar Cheese Sauce.

PLAZA III

CHEDDAR CHEESE SAUCE

1½ cups milk
¼ pound Cheddar cheese,
    cubed
¼ teaspoon paprika
¼ teaspoon dry mustard

½ teaspoon Worcestershire
    sauce
⅛ teaspoon salt
1½ tablespoons butter
3 tablespoons flour

1. Combine milk, cheese, paprika, mustard, Worcestershire, and salt in top of double boiler.
2. Heat until cheese is melted and milk begins to form a skin.
3. Melt butter in a heavy saucepan. Blend in flour and cook 3 to 4 minutes over low heat, stirring constantly to prevent browning.
4. Add to hot milk-and-cheese mixture, whisking until smooth.

This is one of Plaza III's most popular appetizers.

STIR FRY PANACHE

2 tablespoons light peanut
    oil   ½ cup ORIENTAL GLAZE
4 cups seasonal fresh
    vegetables (snow peas,
    thin-sliced; summer
    squash, split and bias
    sliced; fresh red pepper,
    cut into strips; broccoli
    florets; fresh green
    beans, bias sliced; mush-
    rooms, sliced)

1. Heat peanut oil in a large sauté pan or wok until very hot.
2. Add vegetables and toss to heat, but be careful to retain their crispness.
3. Add Glaze to vegetables, toss, and heat thoroughly.

PLAZA III

ORIENTAL GLAZE

2 tablespoons sugar
2 tablespoons cornstarch
1 cup cold water

½ cup soy sauce
3 ounces dry sherry

Combine all ingredients in a saucepan and blend well to dissolve sugar and cornstarch. Bring to a boil. When thick and shiny, remove from stove.

PLAZA III

CHOCOLATISSIMO

20 ounces semi-sweet
  chocolate
2 teaspoons instant coffee

15 ounces unsalted butter
1¼ cups granulated sugar
15 eggs, separated

1. Preheat oven to 350°.
2. In a double boiler, melt chocolate with coffee powder, cool slightly.
3. In a mixing bowl, cream butter and sugar until very light. Add chocolate to creamed butter and blend. Add egg yolks to chocolate mixture one at a time. Mix well after each addition.
4. Whip whites until they form soft peaks and fold by hand into chocolate mixture.
5. Butter 10-inch springform pan. Pour three-quarters of batter into prepared pan and reserve remaining one-quarter of batter at room temperature. Bake for approximately 60 minutes.
6. Remove from oven and allow to cool. The center will fall as cake is cooling. When cool, fill center with reserved filling. Cover and refrigerate until well chilled.
7. Serve thin wedges accompanied by unsweetened whipped cream.

A Restaurant

Dinner for Six

Carpaccio

Skewered Scallops

Linguine with Tomatoes, Vodka, and Caviar

Warm Chèvre Salad
with Cracked Mustard Seed Vinaigrette

Spumoni

Wines:

With Carpaccio—Valpolicella

With Scallops—Chenin Blanc

With Tomatoes, Vodka, and Caviar—Frascati

With Chèvre Salad—Fumé Blanc

With Spumoni—Espresso and Sweet Marsala

Don Anderson, Proprietor

T he Prospect of Westport is a place that transports you for a moment in time to some other place, whether remembered, imagined, or simply enjoyed. Owner-operator Don Anderson is the man responsible for the existence not only of the Prospect but also for Westport Square, a renovated mid-town oasis of retail and entertainment establishments amid courtyards and arcades.

The Prospect seats 125 in an ample space, the focal point of which is an atrium rising two stories skyward, providing light for the profusion of plants and space for the resounding classical music. Natural materials and fresh foods reflect an honesty and sensibility that attract a discriminating and creative clientele. Much of the tile, glass, fabric and brass were acquired in Europe by the architect and the owner, both of whom are Anglophiles.

The sense of freshness, airiness and vitality that characterize the environment also describes the food. A totally à la carte menu offers an eclectic selection of tastes, as the menu says, "to be enjoyed any time of day or evening in sizes and combinations to please your hunger, your mood, your spirit." The menu allows for adventure and experimentation.

"Quality, taste and beautiful presentation are my major concerns," says Bonnie Winston, food and design consultant, who created the menu and the operating philosophy of the restaurant. These elements combined with intelligent service and a beautiful environment make the Prospect a delightful place to dine.

4109 Pennsylvania   753-2227

CARPACCIO

1 pound fillet of beef or eye
 of round, trimmed of all
 fat and sliced paper-thin

MUSTARD MAYONNAISE
¼ cup grated Parmesan
 cheese, preferably
 imported Parmigiano
 Reggiano

Arrange on plate or platter as close to serving time as possible, placing slices in one layer, only slightly overlapping. When ready to serve, drizzle lightly with Mustard Mayonnaise and shred a small amount of good Parmesan over top.

MUSTARD MAYONNAISE

6 egg yolks
1½ cups oil (80% olive oil and
 20% corn oil is our
 preference)
2 tablespoons Dijon
 mustard

1 tablespoon lemon juice,
 freshly squeezed
¼ teaspoon salt
⅛ teaspoon white pepper

1. Beat egg yolks in bowl with wire whisk. Slowly, drop-by-drop at first and then in a slow, steady steam, add oil, whisking all the while.
2. Whisk in mustard, lemon juice, salt, and pepper.

Beef should be so thin as to be nearly transparent; it is easiest to slice if partially frozen and then cut.

Carpaccio is the Italian version of steak tartare; paper-thin slices of lean raw beef sometimes merely drizzled with rich extra-virgin olive oil and perhaps a few grinds of pepper, or dressed with a picante sauce and freshly grated parmigiano reggiano, as served at the Prospect.

SKEWERED SCALLOPS

2 *dozen scallops*
18 *mushrooms, similar in*
  size to scallops

18 *slices ham, very thin,*
  folded in quarters
  to again approximate
  scallops and mushrooms
  in girth
½ *cup butter, melted*
1 *cup grated Parmesan*
  cheese
6 *lime wedges*

1. Thread each skewer as follows: 1 mushroom (stem facing in), folded ham, scallop, ham, scallop, mushroom, scallop, ham, scallop, ham, and mushroom (stem in).
2. Dip skewer in melted butter. Roll in Parmesan cheese.
3. Brown under broiler for about six minutes, or until scallops have become translucent, turning to lightly brown evenly.
4. Add lime wedge to end of skewer.

If using bamboo skewers, soak in water at least 1 hour to prevent burning.

. . . lovely as an appetizer or first course, or perhaps a serving of 2 skewers per person as an entree.

LINGUINE with TOMATOES, VODKA, and CAVIAR

4 tablespoons butter or olive oil
6 cherry tomatoes, halved
4 cloves garlic, pressed or minced fine
½ cup scallions (white & green parts), sliced thin
4 strips lemon rind

¾ cup vodka
1½ cups heavy cream
1 pound egg linguine
Salt and pepper
¼ cup parsley, chopped
¼ cup Parmesan cheese
¼ cup black caviar
Italian parsley

1. Heat butter or oil in sauté pan. Add cherry tomatoes, garlic, scallions, and lemon rind; sauté briefly until tomatoes begin to soften.
2. Add vodka and flame, shaking pan until flame subsides. Add heavy cream and reduce slightly (about 1 minute).
3. While sauce is heating, cook linguine *just* until done in a large quantity of rapidly boiling, salted water. Drain well. Add to sauce immediately along with salt and pepper. Remove from heat, mix well, and transfer to serving bowl.
4. Sprinkle with chopped parsley and Parmesan. Top with caviar in center and garnish with Italian parsley.

WARM CHÈVRE SALAD

Belgian endive
Red leaf lettuce or
* radiccio*
Butter lettuce

Chèvre (goat cheese);
* Montrachet or other goat*
* cheese in log form works*
* well*
Herbes de Provence

1. For each salad, arrange endive spears in the form of a cross so that tips extend slightly beyond edge of plate. Form circle inside spears with red lettuce or radiccio. Form a circle inside red lettuce with light green, tender butter lettuce leaves.
2. Slice chèvre into rounds about 1 inch thick. Place in oven or microwave just until cheese softens; do not melt. Carefully place cheese in center of greens.
3. Sprinkle lightly with herbes de provence. Drizzle Cracked Mustard Seed Vinaigrette over lettuce to dress lightly.

CRACKED MUSTARD SEED VINAIGRETTE

½ cup white wine vinegar
1½ cups olive oil

¼ cup Moutarde de Meaux
Pinch sugar

Whisk ingredients together until thick.

With the growing availability of good goat cheeses, a salad such as this that combines both salad and cheese courses is a lovely transition from entree to dessert.

SPUMONI

1 quart vanilla ice cream
6 tablespoons sweet
  Marsala wine
2 cups heavy cream
6 tablespoons powdered
  sugar
½ teaspoon vanilla

½ cup candied cherries
  (red, or a combination of
  red & green, halved)
½ cup candied pineapple,
  coarsely chopped
2¼ ounces slivered almonds,
  toasted
5 ounces milk chocolate,
  coarsely chopped

1. Soften ice cream in mixer; do not allow to melt. Stir in Marsala wine.
2. Beat cream until stiff, incorporating powdered sugar and vanilla; gently fold into ice cream.
3. Fold in cherries, pineapple, almonds, and chocolate. Ladle into muffin tins that have been lined with foil/paper liners. Freeze immediately, covered.

ROZZELLE COURT

Dinner for Six

Boston Lettuce with Belgian Endive,
Curled Carrots, and Tarragon Cinnamon Vinaigrette

Salmon Fillet en Papillote
with Fresh Vegetable Garnish

Turned Rosemary Potatoes

Pear Sorbet with Poire William, Shaved Chocolate, Sand Tarts

Wine:

Villamont Chassagne Montrachet

Ken Whited, General Manager

Melody Lane, Executive Chef

Ann Lombardi, Menu Development

One would have to look far and wide to find a more handsome setting for a restaurant than that of Rozzelle Court at the Nelson-Atkins Museum of Art. It is a four-story, Italian Renaissance courtyard with a large, marble Roman fountain (circa 128 A.D.) in the center of the court. Tall ficus trees on the perimeter and fresh flowers on the tables create a delightful luncheon atmosphere for the Museum visitor.

It all began twenty-five years ago when a few community-minded volunteers decided to open a small coffee lounge on the mezzanine level of the Nelson-Atkins Museum. They sold coffee and doughnuts in a space that was jointly used as a reading room and lounge.

As years passed, business grew and the menu of the coffee lounge was expanded. A full-time volunteer managed the restaurant and volunteers often delivered dishes prepared in their own kitchens.

The restaurant has come a long way since those early days. A professional manager, Ken Whited, was hired in 1979, and when Rozzelle Court was enclosed with skylights to provide year-round use of the area, it became apparent that the Court was the perfect place for the growing "coffee lounge." Volunteers continue to play an important role in the restaurant service and atmosphere.

The menu is similar to that served in the early days, but with the special culinary and artistic additions of Melody Lane, the restaurant's chef, and Ann Lombardi, the menu developer.

Half sandwiches, hot and cold soups, pastries, and hot entrees are served daily with an emphasis on fresh, seasonal foods. Rozzelle Court offers over thirty wine selections. In addition to luncheon, high tea is served from 2:00 PM to 4:00 PM Tuesday through Friday.

Nelson-Atkins Museum of Art   561-4000
4525 Oak

BOSTON LETTUCE with BELGIAN ENDIVE and CURLED CARROTS

TARRAGON CINNAMON
VINAIGRETTE

3 *heads bib lettuce*
2 *heads Belgian endive*
2 *carrots*

1. Wash lettuce in cold water intact. Pull off outer leaves. Drain well, and cut the head of lettuce exactly in half and remove the core. Place on over-sized plate.
2. Wash Belgian endive and cut the core out.
3. Clean the carrots and slice lengthwise to create three slender strips per carrot. Place each strip in ice water until the carrot has curled.
4. Uncurl the carrot and place five or six pieces of Belgians endive on it. Recurl the carrot strips (by hand). Place the endive and carrot where the core was on the Boston lettuce and chill until served.
5. Serve with Tarragon Cinnamon Vinaigrette.

TARRAGON CINNAMON VINAIGRETTE

1 *shallot*
1 *clove garlic*
½ *teaspoon salt*
1 *cup tarragon vinegar*
¼ *cup minced parsley*

1 *teaspoon fresh tarragon*
½ *teaspoon cinnamon*
1 *teaspoon sugar*
3 *cups peanut oil*

1. Mince shallot and garlic in food processor. Add salt, vinegar, parsley, tarragon, cinnamon, and sugar.
2. Pour oil slowly into food processor with ingredients, blending.

SALMON FILLET EN PAPILLOTE
WITH FRESH VEGETABLE GARNISH

½ pound butter
3 cloves garlic
2 green onions
1 tablespoon fresh tarragon
1 tablespoon fresh chervil
3 large tomatoes, peeled and seeded
3 cups shredded spinach

12 large mushrooms
6 (½-pound) fresh salmon fillets
Salt and fresh-milled black pepper
3 lemons
1 bunch watercress for garnish

1. Preheat oven to 400°.
2. In a large saucepan, melt ¼ pound butter and sauté garlic, green onions, tarragon, chervil, and tomatoes briefly. Set aside.
3. Place a heart-shaped parchment on a work surface and place ⅓ cup shredded spinach, 2 large sliced mushrooms, ⅙ of the sautéed tomato mixture, and one fillet of fresh salmon on one side. Season with salt and pepper. Repeat until all six servings are prepared.
4. Fold the opposite side over the food. Starting at the fold, fold the edge overlapping the fold. As you work your way around the parchment, all the folds made should overlap each other. Fold the tip of the papillote several times to secure the closing. (It is advisable to practice a few times with just parchment.)
5. Bake for 7 minutes. Remove from oven, place on dinner plates, and garnish with lemon flavor and watercress. Serve immediately.

This dish is great for anyone entertaining without help. The Salmon en Papillote can be prepared early in the day and refrigerated until the cooking time.

The real beauty of this entree lies in the parchment itself. When folded correctly, it is sealed so that none of the aroma and steam can escape. The parchment browns nicely and inflates, and the salmon and vegetables inside bake in their own juices. The papillote is served directly on the dinner plate and the guest opens it as a part of dining, with the fragrance embellishing the entree.

TURNED ROSEMARY POTATOES

18 red potatoes
½ cup clarified butter
¼ teaspoon chopped fresh
    rosemary

Salt and freshly milled
black pepper

1. Preheat oven to 400°.
2. Turning potatoes as you pare them, cut each into a 2½-inch olive shape.
3. Sauté the potatoes in the butter until slightly toasted. Place pan and potatoes in oven for another 15 minutes or until tender. Before serving, sprinkle with rosemary and toss lightly with salt and pepper.

ROZZELLE COURT

PEAR SORBET

6 large ripe pears
2 cups water
Juice of ½ lemon
Juice of ½ lime
½–¾ cup sugar

Shaved chocolate, for
  garnish
Poire William Liqueur
SAND TARTS

1. Peel, core, and quarter the pears. Place them in a saucepan and add 2 cups of cold water, lemon and lime juice, and sugar.
2. Poach the pears about 10 minutes until they can be pierced easily with a sharp paring knife. Strain (reserving the liquid) and cool the pears.
3. Puree the pears in a food processor until smooth, adding the reserved liquid to make a quart of the mixture.
4. Pour the puree into the container of a sorbet or ice cream machine and freeze according to the manufacturer's directions.
5. After freezing the sorbet, place in appropriate serving dishes and pour a small amount of Poire William liqueur over just before serving. Sprinkle with shaved chocolate. Serve with Sand Tarts.

SAND TARTS

¼ pound butter	¼ teaspoon salt
2 cups flour	½ tablespoon heavy cream
¾ teaspoon baking soda	½ cup egg whites
½ teaspoon cinnamon	½ cup sugar
1 egg	½ teaspoon cinnamon
1½ cup sugar	40 almonds halves

1. Preheat oven to 325°.
2. Combine the first eight ingredients in the food processor and mix until a ball of dough is formed.
3. Roll the dough into two cylinders 2½ inches thick. Wrap in plastic and refrigerate until firm.
4. Slice the cylinders ¼ inch thick and place on a cookie sheet. Brush each cookie with egg white.
5. Mix the remaining sugar and cinnamon in a separate container, and sprinkle over the cookies. Garnish each cookie with an almond half.
6. Bake for 8 to 10 minutes.

SAVOY GRILL

Dinner for Six

Crabmeat Ravigote

Artichoke Hearts Mimosa

Lobster Thermidor

Mocha Coconut Pie

Wines:

With Crabmeat and Artichokes—Vouvray

With Lobster Thermidor—Pouilly-Fuissé

Don Lee, Owner and General Manager

Andy Brandolese, Executive Chef

By all rights, the Savoy Grill ought to stand on the corner of 12th Street and Vine, the most famous of Kansas City intersections. Residing instead at the corner of 9th and Central since the turn of the century, the Savoy is the matriarch of the city's restaurants, incomparably capturing the flavor and atmosphere of a midwestern city.

Western murals line the walls. Stained-glass windows filter in soft light. A high, beamed ceiling, stained oak paneling, leather booths and brass lanterns give the dining room a spacious, nineteenth-century restaurant saloon effect. In fact, the restaurant and the building that houses it were accepted in 1974 into the National Register of Historic Places.

True to its western ambiance, the restaurant serves highly regarded steaks. Proprietor of the Savoy for twenty-one years, Don Lee proudly claims that his is the only restaurant in town that dry ages its prime meat: "Everyone is now buying what is called 'box-beef,' beef that is vacuum packed and that doesn't shrink in a refrigerator. Dry aging meat in a refrigerator causes shrinkage and is thus uneconomical, but flavor is enhanced."

While Lee boasts about the quality of his meat, the Savoy's pride and joy are lobster and other seafood items. The kitchen contains its own lobster tank, and the restaurant offers the most extensive selection of seafood dishes in town. Either way, steak or seafood, you can't miss at the Savoy.

9th and Central

CRABMEAT RAVIGOTE

4½ cups lump crabmeat
  1 cup RAVIGOTE SAUCE
  1 head lettuce, shredded

2 to 3 tomatoes, depending on
       size, cut into wedges

1. Blend the crabmeat with the Ravigote Sauce, being careful not to break up the crabmeat.
2. Chill in the refrigerator and serve on a bed of shredded lettuce with tomato wedges.

RAVIGOTE SAUCE

  1 cup mayonnaise
1½ tablespoons minced bell
    pepper
1½ tablespoons minced green
    onions

1½ tablespoons minced
    anchovies
1½ tablespoons minced
    pimentos

Mix all ingredients together and chill. This recipe makes 1¼ cups.

NOTE: *The Ravigote Sauce should be prepared at least 8 hours ahead of serving. The key ingredient is the anchovies and they must sit in the mayonnaise for some time to give it their flavor. Prepared mayonnaise is fine here, but do use whole anchovies rather than anchovy paste.*

ARTICHOKE HEARTS MIMOSA

18 canned artichoke hearts,
    drained
1 head of lettuce
1 tablespoon chopped
    pimiento

3 hard-cooked eggs,
    chopped
2 to 3 tomatoes, depending on
    size, cut into wedges
OIL AND VINEGAR
    DRESSING

1. On each of six salad plates, arrange 3 artichoke hearts on a bed of lettuce.
2. Sprinkle on pimiento and eggs.
3. Serve with tomato wedges and Oil and Vinegar Dressing.

OIL AND VINEGAR DRESSING

1 cup olive oil
⅓ cup vinegar
½ teaspoon dry mustard
1 tablespoon chopped
  parsley

½ teaspoon tarragon
½ teaspoon chervil
½ clove shallot, chopped
½ clove garlic, finely minced
  Salt and white pepper

Combine all ingredients and mix well. Shake well before serving.

NOTE: *The dressing for the salad should be prepared a day ahead so the herbs will impart their flavor to the oil and vinegar.*

LOBSTER THERMIDOR

6 (1-pound) lobsters
¼ pound butter
1 cup flour
4 cups milk
¼ bunch green onions, chopped
¼ bunch parsley, chopped
1 large shallot, finely chopped

½ cup coarsely chopped mushrooms
½ teaspoon dry mustard
Salt
½ teaspoon white pepper
½ cup grated Parmesan cheese
¼ cup sherry

1. Boil lobsters approximately 15 minutes in a large kettle of salted water.
2. Let them cool, then split in half and remove the lobster meat. Cut meat in large chunks.
3. Melt butter in a saucepan. Add flour, stirring over low heat for 2 minutes. Remove from heat and pour in the milk. Stir well to mix with flour and butter. Return sauce to heat and bring to boil. Remove from heat.
4. Add remaining ingredients to the sauce, reserving 2 tablespoons Parmesan.
5. Mix well, then add the chopped lobster meat.
6. Preheat oven to 250°.
7. Stuff lobster shells and dust with remaining Parmesan cheese.
8. Bake for 10 minutes in preheated oven.

NOTE: The sauce for Lobster Thermidor has to be thick because it must stay in the shell. If the sauce is too thin when it is heated, it will run. It should be sharp tasting and heavy enough to stand on your finger.

MOCHA COCONUT PIE

1¼ cups canned sweet
   shredded coconut
2 ounces unsweetened
   chocolate
2 tablespoons brandy
2 tablespoons instant
   coffee powder
½ pound unsalted butter,
   softened

½ cup sugar
2 large eggs
½ cup ground hazelnuts
½ cup ground blanched
   almonds
1 cup heavy cream, whipped
   and sweetened with 2
   tablespoons sugar

1. Line the bottom and sides of an 8-inch pie plate with shredded coconut and bake in a 250° oven for 1 hour or until golden.
2. Transfer the pie plate to a rack and let the shell cool.
3. In the top of a double boiler set over hot water, melt unsweetened chocolate with brandy and instant coffee.
4. Cream together unsalted butter and sugar. Beat in eggs, 1 at a time, beating well after each addition.
5. Add the chocolate mixture, hazelnuts, and almonds.
6. Transfer the filling to the shell and chill the pie for at least 3 hours.
7. Serve each slice with a dab of whipped cream.

Dinner for Six

Chicken Noodle Soup

Chicken-Fried Steak

Cottage Fries

Biscuits

Brandy Ice

Wine:

Mouton-Cadet Blanc

James Hogan, Dennis Donegan, and Michael Donegan, Owners

Chris McSorley and Larry Hunt, Kitchen Managers

STROUD'S

Often a restaurant's decor can contribute almost as much to the enjoyment of a fine meal as the food itself. Other establishments forget that without good food the decor becomes an unnecessary pretext. Happily, Stroud's combines both with fantastic results.

At very reasonable prices, the dinner menu offers a large selection of pan-fried chicken ("The best in the world," say the owners modestly), barbequed ribs, Kansas City strip steaks, pan-fried catfish, and pan-fried pork chops, all served in large portions with soup or salad, vegetables, and potatoes of your choice with pan-fried gravy. The homemade cinnamon rolls are truly a taste treat.

The owners, Jim Hogan, Dennis Donegan, and Mike Donegan, have tastefully and succesfully combined their love for antiques and the antiquated in a setting which makes for a truly different dining experience. The building itself is not exactly Early American or even Victorian. If your table is listing to port or starboard, it is not due to the improper adjustments of its legs: it is probably one of the Stroud's treasures. The antiques are very tastefully placed on the walls, behind the bar, and hanging from the ceiling. If the paraphernalia doesn't fascinate you, just relax at the table and enjoy Helen Bess's piano, and perhaps join in the sing-along of America's old tunes.

Stroud's
1015 East 85th Street
333-2132

Stroud's Oak Ridge Manor
5410 N.E. Oak Ridge Road
454-9600

CHICKEN NOODLE SOUP

4 quarts water
2 chicken breasts
2 chicken thighs
2 tablespoons chicken soup
   base (bouillon cubes can
   be substituted)
   Pinch of oregano

Salt and pepper to taste
1 (12-ounce) package
   Reames egg noodles
1 stalk celery, chopped
1 tablespoon onion
1 tablespoon chopped carrot

1. Bring water to boil. Drop in chicken breasts and thighs. Add soup base, oregano, and salt and pepper to taste. Boil for 1 hour. Remove chicken pieces and set aside.
2. Add noodles and chopped celery and onion and carrot. Bring to boil again and simmer for 30 minutes.
3. De-bone chicken breasts and thighs and dice the meat. Add meat to stock and serve.

Mr. Hunt makes his noodles from scratch but has found frozen Reames egg noodles to be a very good substitute.

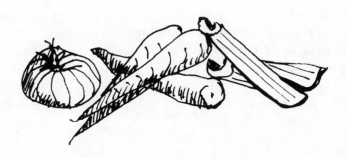

CHICKEN-FRIED STEAK

Salt and pepper
1 tablespoon paprika
2 cups flour
1 egg

4 cups milk
6 (5- to 6-ounce) cubed
  steaks
GRAVY

1. Add salt, pepper, and paprika to the flour.
2. Beat the egg and mix with milk to make a batter.
3. Dredge each steak thoroughly in seasoned flour and then dip into the batter of milk and egg.
4. Dredge each steak again in flour and pound out with a meat mallet to tenderize. This breaks down any coarse meat tissues.
5. Heat a well-greased griddle or heavy skillet until hot but not smoking. Add steaks and cook until golden brown on both sides.
6. To serve, pour Gravy over steaks.

GRAVY

Cracklings of Chicken-
  Fried Steak
6 tablespoons flour

3 cups milk
Salt and pepper

1. Cover the bottom ½ inch of a medium-size frying pan with the cracklings and grease left from the fried meat.
2. Spoon in flour and stir until it has the appearance of paste.
3. Bring to a boil. Slowly add milk.
4. Cook slowly until the gravy returns to a boil, stirring constantly to keep the gravy from sticking to bottom of the pan. Season to taste.

A whisk is very helpful for blending the milk into the flour and drippings. Stirring with the whisk prevents lumps from forming.

COTTAGE FRIES

8 *large Idaho potatoes*   *Salt and pepper*

1. Preheat deep-fat fryer to 360°.
2. Peel and slice the potatoes lengthwise. Pat dry on paper towels.
3. Drop the potatoes into preheated deep-fat fryer and cook until crisp and golden brown.
4. Pat off grease; add salt and pepper to taste.

What makes these special is using Idaho potatoes instead of red potatoes. Try leaving the skins on for a new twist.

BISCUITS

3 cups flour   ¼ cup sugar
3 teaspoons baking powder   1 cup cold shortening
2 tablespoons salt   1¾ cups cold milk

1. Preheat oven to 450°.
2. Combine dry ingredients in a bowl. Cut in shortening with a pastry blender.
3. Add cold milk and stir until the batter cleans the sides of the bowl and the dough forms a ball. If dough is too dry, add small amount of milk until dough can be rolled out.
4. Pat out ½-inch thick; let rise 30 minutes. Cut with biscuit cutter and place close together on a greased baking sheet.
5. Bake for 15 minutes.

NOTE: *If you prefer a crisp biscuit, do not place them close together and they will brown on all sides.*

BRANDY ICE

6   scoops vanilla ice cream
¾ cup brandy

¾ cup dark crème de cacao
Nutmeg

1. Place ice cream, brandy and crème de cacao in a blender. Blend until the mixture has the consistency of a thick malt.
2. Serve in large champagne glasses with a pinch of nutmeg on top.

The trick to this dessert is to keep your guests from having too many seconds.

Dinner for Four

Mussel Soup

Tatsu's House Salad

Stuffed Sole in Pieshell

Cheesecake

Wines:

With Stuffed Sole—Chardonnay

Tatsuya Aria, Proprietor/Chef

TATSU'S

Tatsu got his start working in a French restaurant, Kokeshiya, in Tokyo at the age of sixteen. There he studied cooking until he decided to come to the United States four years later.

Since then he has worked at places like the Bastille, Maxims, and La Festival. Tatsu came to Kansas City to work with the Hibachi restaurant in the Country Club Plaza. Two years later, he got his independence by opening up his own restaurant which is located in Prairie Village.

Tatsu's consists of two small, simply decorated rooms. Wooden panels set the stage for the exquisite dishes typical of French and Japanese cuisine. Dishes are prepared individually with particular attention and care, even down to the tiniest details.

Note: To accommodate customer's demands for wine to accompany their meals, Tatsu's is now serving as a private club. Memberships are available upon request.

4603 W. 90th   383-3858

MUSSEL SOUP

2 pounds mussels, well
   scrubbed
2 shallots, minced
½ onion, chopped
½ cup white wine
1 bay leaf

Pinch of thyme
2 cups clam juice
3 tablespoons arrowroot
   or cornstarch
½ cup heavy cream

1. Cook mussels, shallots, onions, white wine, bay leaf, and thyme over high heat. Shake several times to open mussel shells. Set mussels to one side after straining them for juice.
2. Combine mussel juice with clam juice and arrowroot. Heat to boil.
3. Place mussels in the above broth and season to taste.
4. Add cream to soup before turning off heat. Do not overcook after cream has been added. Serve soup with a little bit of chives in center.

TATSU'S HOUSE SALAD

1 egg yolk	¼ cup red wine vinegar
1 tablespoon Dijon mustard	1 cup salad oil
½ tablespoon salt	1 tablespoon soy sauce
⅔ tablespoon black pepper	Lettuce, cleaned and cut
1 small clove garlic, minced	into bite-size pieces

1. In mixing bowl, combine egg yolk, mustard, salt, pepper, and garlic.
2. Add vinegar and oil alternately to egg yolk mixture. Finally, add soy sauce. Dressing is complete when it is creamy in texture.
3. Toss with lettuce to coat all the lettuce before serving.

NOTE: This salad dressing may be used for any type of salad.

TATSU'S

STUFFED SOLE IN PIESHELL

4 (6–8 ounce) sole fillets	SEAFOOD MOUSSE
1 shallot, thinly sliced	PASTRY
4 large mushrooms, cut into strips	CHAMPAGNE SAUCE

1. Preheat oven to 425°.
2. Enlarge the size of the sole fillet by cutting sideways into the fillets. Season with salt and pepper.
3. Sauté shallot in butter. Add mushrooms and cook until slightly brown. Cool.
4. Divide Mousse evenly on to sole fillets. Top Mousse with mushrooms. Shape sole fillets into oval pieces.
5. Roll out pastry to ⅛-inch thickness. Divide into eight pieces (these should measure 6 × 9½ inches each).
6. Place sole in the center of pastry. Top with another piece of pastry. Shape and seal off the edges. Cut into the shape of a fish. Decorate as desired.
7. Bake for 20 minutes. Serve with Champagne Sauce.

SEAFOOD MOUSSE

1 pound scallops, shrimp, salmon, sole, mixed	Salt and pepper
1 egg	1 teaspoon cognac
	½ cup heavy cream

1. Blend seafood in food processor. Add egg, salt, pepper, and cognac. Mix well.
2. Refrigerate at least half an hour.
3. In a bowl, add cream to mousse a little at a time. Mix well with a spatula. (It is better to do this when mousse is placed over a large bowl full of ice.)
4. Refrigerate mousse at least half an hour before using.

PASTRY

2-2½ cups flour	½ pound cold, fresh butter
Pinch of salt	⅓ cup cold water

1. Sift flour and salt directly on to pastry board.
2. Cut butter into small cubes and place in center of flour.
3. Mix well. Add water and roll into a rectangle (about 18 inches × 12 inches). Fold in thirds. Repeat this process about four times. Refrigerate at least 15 minutes after each roll.
4. Refrigerate at least one hour before use.

TATSU'S

CHAMPAGNE SAUCE

¾ cup FISH STOCK
¼ cup champagne
¼ cup white wine (if champagne is not available, use ½ cup white wine)

1 shallot, minced
2 mushrooms, sliced
1½ cups heavy cream
Salt and pepper
1 teaspoon butter
1 teaspoon flour

1. Combine stock, Champagne, white wine, shallots, and mushrooms. Cook until liquid is reduced to ¼ cup.
2. Add cream, cook, and reduce to 1¼ cups.
3. Salt and pepper to taste. To thicken sauce, combine 1 teaspoon butter and 1 teaspoon flour. Add to sauce.

Excess fish stock can be frozen and can be used in almost every kind of cooking that calls for fish.

TATSU'S

FISH STOCK

3 pounds fish bones, cleaned
6 cups water
1 cup white wine
   Pinch of salt
10 white peppercorns
½ onion

1 carrot
2 shallots, optional
1 small celery stalk
1 bay leaf
   Pinch of thyme

Cook all ingredients first over high heat then simmer for 30 minutes. Strain slowly.

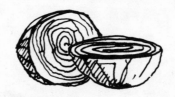

CHEESECAKE

12 ounces cream cheese
¾ cup sugar
1¼ envelope Knox gelatin
¼ cup milk
3 egg yolks

Juice of ½ large lemon
1 cup heavy cream
1 teaspoon triple sec
SPONGE CAKE

1. Melt cream cheese in double boiler. Add sugar.
2. In separate bowl, combine gelatin and milk. Add to cream cheese mixture.
3. Add egg yolk and lemon juice. Whip until thick and creamy. Strain and cool.
4. Whip heavy cream until soft peaks form. Fold gently into cheese mixture. Add triple sec.
5. Pour into 7-inch round cake pan and cool. Top with prepared Sponge Cake. To serve, invert onto plate. Serve with whipped cream.

SPONGE CAKE

4 eggs
¼ cup butter
½ cup sugar

⅛ cup milk
1 cup flour

1. Preheat to 375°.
2. Beat eggs and butter until thick. Add sugar and milk. Mix well until texture is thick and creamy.
3. Add flour all at once. It is best to mix flour in by hand.
4. Prepare a 7-inch round cake pan by lining side and bottom with wax paper. Pour in cake mixture. Bake for 20 minutes. Cake is done when it springs back when touched with finger.

TOP OF THE TOWN.
TOP OF THE CROWN.

Dinner for Four

Timbale of Rock Lobster with Cold Spiced Tomato Sauce

Sautéed Veal Chops with Ginger and Hazelnut Sauce

Baby Turnips, Pea Pods, and Miniature Crookneck Squash

*Redicchio and Belgium Endive
with Blueberry Vinegar Dressing*

Blackberry Tart

Wines:

With Appetizer and Salad, 1982 Stags Leap-Chenin Blanc

With Veal Chops and Salad, 1980 Kenwood Chardonnay

With Dessert, 1982 Chateau-Ste. Michelle Johannisberg Riesling

*James E. Durham, Vice President and Managing Director
Hans Bruland, Director of Food and Beverage
Michael Glennon, Maitre D'—Top of the Crown
Peter Inauen, Executive Chef
Martin Uddenberg, Chef de Cuisine*

The Top of the Crown offers the ultimate in exquisite fine dining, dancing, and superb service for Kansas Citians and visitors alike. The restaurant is perched atop The Westin Crown Center Hotel, high above the tropical garden and cascading five-story indoor waterfall.

While dining at the Top of the Crown, you will enjoy a panoramic view of Kansas City and personalized table service as you relax in the tastefully designed, elegant room which gives one a comfortable feeling of regalness and charm. To have fun relaxing or dancing, the restaurant's lounge atmosphere provides the perfect informal setting to enjoy live entertainment which is offered nightly.

Continental and nouvelle dishes are expertly prepared by the Chef de Cuisine, Martin Uddenberg, and carefully supervised by European-trained Executive Chef Peter Inauen. Martin Uddenberg comes to the Top of the Crown having served his apprenticeship in San Francisco at The Westin St. Francis, and most recently as Sou Chef at the famous five-star restaurant, Palm Court, at The Westin Seattle in Washington.

The resplendence of the Top of the Crown is an integral part of The Westin Crown Center's total environment and provides the perfect setting for a most memorable dining experience for all special occasions.

The Top of the Crown has been awarded the Silver Spoon Award by Outlook, and has been the recipient of many other honors and awards for food service and quality.

Sunday Brunch at the Top of the Crown is an exquisite dining experience. The brunch is noted for a most complete selection of specialty prepared items not only as breakfast/brunch entrees, but as a gourmet fare, unmatched in Kansas City.

1 Crown Center   474-4400
1 Pershing Road

TIMABLE OF ROCK LOBSTER

1 *(8-ounce) rock lobster tail*	1 *tablespoon brandy*
½ *cup FISH STOCK*	1 *leaf gelatin*
2 *tablespoons white wine*	*COLD SPICED TOMATO*
1½ *cups whipping cream*	*SAUCE*
Salt and white pepper	

1. Poach lobster in Fish Stock and white wine. Remove cooked lobster and reduce stock until lightly thickened.
2. Puree lobster meat, adding reduced stock, whipping cream, salt and white pepper, and brandy, until it becomes a smooth mixture.
3. Dissolve gelatin in cold water.
4. Whip heavy cream.
5. Fold lobster mixture, whipped cream, and gelatin together until mixed. Place mixture into molds, cover, and chill.
6. Place Tomato Sauce on 9-inch plate, place lobster mousse on sauce, garnish with such as crawfish, truffle, or watercress leaves.

FISH STOCK

3 *pounds fish bones, cleaned*	1 *carrot*
6 *cups water*	2 *shallots, optional*
Pinch of salt	1 *small celery stalk*
10 *white peppercorns*	1 *bay leaf*
½ *onion*	*Pinch of thyme*

Cook all ingredients first over high heat, then simmer for 30 minutes. Strain slowly.

COLD SPICED TOMATO SAUCE

4 shallots
Butter
4 tomatoes, peeled and
   seeded

3-4 tablespoons tomato paste
Salt and pepper
Thyme

1. Sauté shallots in butter. Add peeled tomatoes and tomato paste. Add salt, pepper, and thyme.
2. Puree in food processor or blender. Chill until needed.

SAUTÉED VEAL CHOPS with GINGER & HAZELNUT DRESSING

4 (8-ounce) veal chops
Salt and pepper
Flour
¼ cup butter + 1 tablespoon
1½ cup white wine
½ cup dry vermouth

3 cups brown sauce (use
   packet Brown Sauce,
   such as Knorr)
½ cup finely sliced ginger
1 cup coarsely chopped
   hazelnuts

1. Preheat oven to 325°–350°.
2. Trim excess fat and tendons from veal chops and season both sides with salt and white pepper. Dust both sides with flour.
3. Heat a ¼ cup of butter in a sauté pan, and place veal chops into it. Sauté until golden brown on both sides and add 1 cup white wine, dry vermouth, and brown sauce.
4. Place in oven, covered. Turn the chops every 5 minutes. Remove from the oven and take the veal chops out of the sauce and keep warm.
5. Heat 1 tablespoon of butter in a saucepan until light brown. Add ginger and hazelnuts and toss for a few seconds. Add ½ cup white wine and bring to a boil. Add the brown sauce from the veal chops. Simmer for about 3–4 minutes. Adjust seasoning and set aside.

TOP OF THE CROWN

BABY TURNIPS, PEA PODS, AND MINIATURE CROOKNECK SQUASH

4 *whole miniature turnips*
   with stem
4 *(1½–2") little crookneck*
   squash

16 *fresh pea pods*
    Butter
    Salt and pepper

1. Cook turnips and squash in boiling, salted water. When soft, remove and plunge in cold water.
2. Sauté pea pods, squash, and turnips in lightly browned butter. Season with salt and pepper.
3. On a dinner plate, arrange the vegetables with the pea pods on top of the plate, right beside the squash and left of the turnips that have been cut lengthwise in half.
4. Place veal chops in the middle and lace with the sauce.
5. Sprinkle chopped parsley or chives on top.

REDICCHIO AND BELGIUM ENDIVE
WITH BLUEBERRY VINEGAR DRESSING

2 heads of redicchio lettuce
1 Belgium endive
4 shredded radishes

½ pint alfalfa sprouts
BLUEBERRY VINEGAR
DRESSING

Separate redicchio lettuce and Belgium endive into leaves. Wash in cold water, shake dry, and arrange on plate with alfalfa sprouts in center. Sprinkle with shredded radishes. Drizzle with Dressing.

BLUEBERRY VINEGAR DRESSING

1 whole egg
1 shallot, finely chopped
Pinch of salt
Pinch of white pepper

2 teaspoons sugar
½ cup blueberry vinegar
1½ cup salad oil

Place the whole egg and chopped shallots into a bowl, add the salt, pepper, and sugar. Mix it well with a whisk and slowly add the oil and vinegar together. Adjust seasoning if necessary.

BLACKBERRY TART

1 (9") baked pie shell	4 cups blackberries
2 cups PASTRY CREAM	Sugar
	Whipping cream

Spread cold pastry cream into pie shell evenly and place blackberries upright on top. Sprinkle with sugar and garnish with the whipping cream.

PASTRY CREAM

2 cups milk	4 egg yolks
⅓ teaspoon vanilla	1½ tablespoons flour
2 tablespoons sugar	

1. Boil milk with vanilla and half the sugar.
2. Mix egg yolk and other half of sugar together; add flour.
3. Add some hot milk over egg yolk mixture and, after mixing it well, pour it back into the pot with the remaining hot milk. Bring to a boil for about 1 minute. Remove and cool.

RECIPE INDEX

Appetizers

Desserts and Accents

RECIPE INDEX

Entrées

Pasta, Rice and Bread

Beverages

Salad Dressings

Salads

DINING IN–THE GREAT CITIES
A Collection of Gourmet Recipes from the Finest Chefs in the Country

Each book contains gourmet recipes for complete meals from the chefs of 21 great restaurants.

____ *Dining In–Baltimore*	$7.95	____ *Dining In–Monterey Peninsula*	$7.95
____ *Dining In–Boston (Revised)*	8.95	____ *Dining In–Philadelphia*	8.95
____ *Dining In–Chicago, Vol. II*	8.95	____ *Dining In–Phoenix*	8.95
____ *Dining In–Chicago, Vol. III*	8.95	____ *Dining In–Pittsburgh (Revised)*	7.95
____ *Dining In–Cleveland*	8.95	____ *Dining In–Portland*	7.95
____ *Dining In–Dallas (Revised)*	8.95	____ *Dining In–St. Louis*	7.95
____ *Dining In–Denver*	7.95	____ *Dining In–San Francisco, Vol. II*	8.95
____ *Dining In–Hawaii*	8.95	____ *Dining In–Seattle, Vol. III*	8.95
____ *Dining In–Houston, Vol. II*	7.95	____ *Dining In–Sun Valley*	7.95
____ *Dining In–Kansas City (Revised)*	8.95	____ *Dining In–Toronto*	8.95
____ *Dining In–Los Angeles (Revised)*	8.95	____ *Dining In–Vail*	8.95
____ *Dining In–Manhattan*	8.95	____ *Dining In–Vancouver, B.C.*	8.95
____ *Dining In–Milwaukee*	8.95	____ *Dining In–Washington, D.C.*	8.95
____ *Dining In–Minneapolis/St. Paul, Vol. II* .	8.95		

☐ Check (✔) here is you would like to have a different Dining In–Cookbook sent to you once a month. Payable by MasterCard or VISA. Returnable if not satisfied.

Please include $1.00 postage and handling for each book.

☐ Payment enclosed $ _____ (total amount)

☐ Charge to:

VISA # _____   Exp. Date _____

MasterCard # _____   Exp. Date _____

Signature _____

Name _____

Address _____

City _____   State _____ Zip _____

SHIP TO (if other than name and address above):

Name _____

Address _____

City _____   State _____ Zip _____

PEANUT BUTTER PUBLISHING
2445 76th Avenue S.E. ▪ Mercer Island, WA 98040 ▪ (206) 236-1982

KAN
11/83